# Crimes Against Data

## 101 true crime stories of people abusing and misusing data

## Merrill Albert

Technics Publications

Published by:

115 Linda Vista, Sedona, AZ 86336 USA
https://www.TechnicsPub.com

Edited by Sadie Hoberman
Cover design by Lorena Molinari

First Printing 2023
Copyright © 2023 by Merrill Albert

| ISBN, print ed. | 9781634623476 |
| --- | --- |
| ISBN, Kindle ed. | 9781634623483 |
| ISBN, ePub ed. | 9781634623513 |
| ISBN, PDF ed. | 9781634623537 |

Library of Congress Control Number: 2023940875

This is a book about true crime stories of people abusing and misusing data. As the saying goes, those who do not learn history are doomed to repeat it. If we don't document and understand these stories, we can't learn from them and prevent them from happening again.

This book is for people who want to finally understand why organizations keep making mistakes. It's also for data people who need some stories to explain the importance of getting the data right. Or to laugh and reminisce.

---

*This book is dedicated to everyone who defends data.*
*It can't take care of itself.*
*We need to look after it.*

# Contents at a Glance

# Contents

# Introduction

When I witness people misusing data, I call it a "data crime." This quickly progressed to me creating the hashtag "#CrimesAgainstData," which you'll find attached to some of my posts on LinkedIn. Someone pointed out that it wasn't so much a crime against data as it was a crime against me! That is somewhat true, although not all stories I relate are personal to me. Some are stories I hear about from others. It might be more of a crime against someone based on data.

Data crimes are unnecessary. Why do we have data crimes? Perhaps some people are being careless and are trying to do something quickly. Perhaps some people haven't been trained in good data principles. For the most part, people probably aren't thinking through how their actions might impact others. They don't realize how a little thing like data can have far-reaching implications.

Data crimes can be about people misusing data or people creating bad data. Data crimes can have operational or analytical impacts. If you don't have a correct address for a customer and a truckload of perishable goods can't be delivered, your data crime has a huge impact. The truckload of goods goes to waste, you might have to send another load, and there is an impact to your customer relationship. If gender is a missing data point on many of your customer records and you're trying to do analytics using that data, that data crime will impact your results. The decisions you make based on those results could be wrong and affect a significant number of your customers.

Think through the implications of what you're doing. Do you have the right data to reach your customer? Do you make up data that might offend your customer? If you think bad data is statistically insignificant, have you proven that?

Why are all these data crimes happening? I think it comes down to education. Do people really understand how to properly treat their data? Data management requires some structured knowledge. You do not learn this from attending a one-hour seminar or a one-week vendor course, reading a book, or watching YouTube videos. Those can help give you a base to work from or reinforce your training, but you want to make sure you're not taking a narrow view of data. You need to understand the big picture.

I titled an earlier version of this book, "Stories I Tell My Data Friends." That was because I shared a lot of these stories with my data friends – the ones with a data background who got how I looked at these stories from a data perspective. I later realized that the non-data people probably needed these stories more. A story might better help them make sense out of what is happening to them, rather than someone making a generic statement telling them they need data management. Ultimately though, we should all understand the power of data.

Hopefully, reading these data crimes will help you better understand the importance of data. I also try to get into the minds of the offenders to figure out what they were thinking to help you identify data crimes when you see them and prevent data crimes of your own. Hopefully, these stories will also put a smile on your face. Unfortunately, the smile often comes in hindsight because dealing with data crimes can be frustrating. What data crimes have you been the victim of?

# The Origin Story

I was once in line at the self-checkout of a large national retailer. As I waited my turn, I saw a woman buying a package of white hangers and a package of blue hangers. She asked the employee if she had to ring them up separately. The employee told her they were the same, so she didn't need to. As a data person, and a data person who has consulted at this particular retailer, I knew the employee answered the question incorrectly. Of course it mattered! They were different colors, so they had different SKUs and needed to be scanned separately. I didn't bring it to their attention and let them mess up their own inventory.

A few weeks later, I was back at the same retailer in the same line. I assume the people involved were different, but the scenario was the same. This time, someone was trying to buy multiple cases of Coke. She asked the employee if she had to ring them up separately. This time, the employee told her it was fine if they truly were all Coke, but if something was Diet Coke or Sprite, she had to ring them up separately. Yes! The data was preserved!

When I was telling people about the second situation, I said that I had returned to the scene of the data crime. From there, it was easy to make up the hashtag #CrimesAgainstData. However, like all good data people, I checked to see if anyone was already using that hashtag to make sure that my references would mean what I intended them to mean. Isn't being a data person exhausting?

## CHAPTER 1

# Crimes Against Addresses

## Trust Me – I Know My Address

I had a longstanding case open with a large global hotel chain that couldn't get my address right. Initially, I was willing to blame it on myself for entering the address incorrectly, but then I easily noticed that I could change my address every day, it would look correct in the application that day, and then be wrong the next day. And I'm not talking about a little wrong. I'm talking about them changing my address to "36 C." How does the United States Postal Service (USPS) deliver mail to "36 C"?

When I first started calling the hotel chain, employees tried to change the address, and it would be fine on the screen, but then it would be "36 C" the next day. Obviously, they have some program running on a nightly basis that standardizes addresses. This is a fairly common practice. Customer Care can enter addresses, and then things get standardized to how the organization wants to use addresses. It could be something like changing "Road" to

"Rd." It could be splitting a street address and a unit number across separate address lines.

Perhaps addresses might be considered too long and the address standardization uses some common abbreviations. But really, is there a reason a database has such short address lines in today's day and age? Some databases support variable lengths rather than a fixed length, where some space goes to waste. I'm assuming that this particular hotel chain decided that my address line was too long. It wasn't outrageous, but probably longer than average. However, what would possess them to truncate my address to "36 C" – four characters? They've got some bizarre rules going on. Did the business approve truncating addresses to four characters? Was 30 or 20 characters not ok? Did this pass testing before going into production?

Anyway, this is a long-winded way to say that I started debugging their problem. They opened three cases in attempts to fix it over a period of months. How did it get fixed? I honestly don't know. It was just suddenly correct one day and stayed correct. I joked that they had put in a special line of code not to change my address. When I next moved, I looked forward to seeing if they would let me change my address and they did. I haven't had problems with them since.

## Updating Addresses Repetitively

I have multiple policies with a global insurance company and they got my address wrong in different ways on each policy. Ideally, my address should be tied to all my policies so I can just go online, update my address once, and everything is good. I was shocked that a company their size didn't obviously have a customer master that allowed me to do that. Mastering data is really important. At the very least, even if you don't know or follow the concept of "mastering," you can better manage your data to make it easier on everyone.

It was interesting to see how Customer Care handled the situation. They were surprised as well that they had to update my address in multiple places, but it got even more complicated. Their application felt my address was too long, so they tried lots of tricks to update it. Once they fixed it in one place, they didn't remember what they did and tried something else in another place. At one point, one of my policies had my street address appended to my last name, but USPS seemed able to deliver mail to me. I didn't change my name!

I suppose problems like that sometimes happen when a company acquires another company, but I would have thought they would have had something that important worked out pretty quickly. Addresses are something that most organizations need to deal with and the basic structure hasn't changed in a long time. This is something solved decades ago.

The next time I moved, I called the company, and the employee updated my address very quickly. Too quickly. I asked about the prior issue and she said it was no longer an issue. It was. The next time I got mail, I saw that they didn't update all policies and I had to call them back. I eventually got one of the more experienced employees who knew what this newer employee had done wrong. It was an ordeal that lasted a period of time before resolution.

## Address Rules

A company struggled with my address, claiming it was too long. No matter what Customer Care did, the application wasn't accepting my address. I made some suggestions for shortening my address or abbreviating certain words, but nothing we tried worked. If their rules had been documented somewhere and accessible, we could have constructed an address that fit those rules. A case study on the value of documenting your rules! Plus, fix the database so it isn't so restrictive. My address wasn't that long.

Business rules need to come from the business. Technology should support the rules, but IT shouldn't be left figuring them out. Also, technology staff sometimes get outsourced to other countries where business rules can be different. Something as simple as addresses can be constructed differently in different countries. The business rules also need to be validated by the business before going into production.

I like to think that had anyone asked, someone would have brought up the fact that the address length was far too restrictive. Even if we assume the business validated the length as appropriate, since it was not documented, no one could look it up. I was trying to help them, but this really wasn't my problem to debug.

In addition to documenting and validating pre-production, business rules aren't always static. There needs to be a process to review them on a regular basis. While it would be great to think that a team would examine the rules if something happens, it is also likely that some things will slip through the cracks but can be caught in a yearly review. When it falls under my control, I do a yearly review and then schedule the next yearly review on my calendar.

# The 2020 United States Census

Several weeks after receiving a form about the 2020 census and completing it online, I received another form in the mail. Since a significant period of time had passed, I took a better look. Every census address has a unique ID and I saw that this second form had a different ID than the first one. Then I noticed that the address was slightly different, using different abbreviations for words and using different city names. Both were valid addresses for me, but they were the same location and didn't warrant two separate census forms.

Census information determines the number of seats in Congress. It determines funding for schools, roads, and public services. Family history researchers will use it in 72 years. Not filling out a census form gets you nastygrams from the government that start sounding increasingly serious as time passes. It's also highly unlikely mine was the only address with a problem, although I don't know the magnitude of the problem. Everyone on my street and region might have had the same problem.

Based on what happened, it's clear that the government pulled address data from multiple places. What surprises me is that they didn't recognize and reconcile the addresses. I would have expected that the government already maintains a clean list, such as with the Tax Assessor, but apparently not.

I took the time to understand the issue, but I'm sure most people didn't. Some people probably filled out the second form forgetting they had filled out the first one or did not know that someone else in the household had filled it out. Some people probably threw out the second form knowing they had filled out the first one, but then continued getting nastygrams from the government and risked a personal visit from a census worker during a pandemic. The government might have had to employ additional census workers depending on the magnitude of this problem.

Although for the 2020 census, this problem probably wasn't new. Unless the government revamped its applications for the 2020 census, this problem existed in prior census data and decisions were made based upon erroneous data.

# How Long is that Power Cord?

Sometimes, we must do our own testing. Never underestimate an organization's ability to mess up your data! I had a personal assistant device that seemed to give some questionable answers after I moved. It didn't seem to know what state it was in. It would answer some questions (e.g., weather) based on its new location, but some questions (e.g., distance) based on its old location. Tech support suggested unplugging it, which I obviously did over 1,000 miles previously. It was surprising how many times they suggested I unplug it.

After they finally accepted where I lived, they continued researching the issue. It turned out that they maintained location information in multiple places. I had updated my address when I moved, but I had updated it only in the place that seemed logical. I wasn't aware that an additional super-secret place also retained my address.

This was a bad design on their part, but also something Tech Support wasn't really aware of. I had to go through multiple Tech Support employees before finding one who recognized that I had only updated my address in one place rather than the two they required. I have since made a note of it for my next move.

## Personal Assistant Device

Following from the previous story, the personal assistant device wasn't always giving accurate answers because it didn't consistently know where it was. The device answered some questions based on location stored in one place and some questions were answered based on location stored somewhere else. The technology isn't good enough to resolve that discrepancy. And yet, we see that people trust it enough to take information into court proceedings.

It's interesting to see how quickly people adapted to personal assistant devices, even though most use them just for music. We have to understand what they're capable of and what they're not capable of. It comes down to the underlying data.

When something as simple as the location is inconsistent, you must check more complicated data to know if you can trust that. Is it accurately tracking what it's done? Is its history complete? Does it accurately capture recordings? Does it hear questions correctly? Understanding the validity of the data is important before trusting it legally.

# A ZIP Code is not Numeric

Another "good" data crime is truncating leading zeroes. Sometimes you don't need a leading zero, but sometimes you do. If you decide to store a ZIP Code as numeric, you risk losing your leading zero, and some places have ZIP Codes that start with a zero.

Leading zeroes don't matter on fields that are truly numbers that you're doing math on. We want "100." We don't need "0100," although the math is the same. We're not doing math on ZIP Codes.

People sometimes keep the ZIP+4 Code, which includes a hyphen, so that also wouldn't be numeric. However, most people ignore the "+4," so a ZIP Code looks numeric. You really need to understand your data. It doesn't take too much research to determine that there can be leading zeroes that will always get dropped in certain applications. ZIP Codes have been around for decades, so this should be known by now. It's not a problem we have to keep solving.

I am curious about this because I don't know what the USPS does when they encounter a ZIP Code of length 4. Do they assume there's a missing zero, or do they reject it as a bad ZIP Code and don't deliver the mail?

## Where Do You Live?

I had an account with a food delivery app that wouldn't accept my home address in my account. I could enter the address as a delivery address, but not as a home address. When I tried, it either said my address wasn't valid or it changed my street number. I could also try to update my address on my phone and my laptop, getting different responses on each device. This is a great example of a company not using, or not consistently using, a location master. It stored my address in multiple places, rather than letting me enter it once.

You can definitely live at one location and order food to another location. We've probably all seen websites where we order something, enter the ship-to address, and then have a checkbox to say if the bill-to address is the same, thus saving us from entering it a second time. This food delivery app was not doing that.

In this particular case, I had moved to a new development, so not all companies knew about the address yet. What was unusual was that it accepted the address depending on where I was in this app, but other places in the same app decided that it didn't exist. I just wanted my food!

# Maps

I was working with a company that was so proud of its search engine tied to Google Maps. A customer could start entering an address and their application would start prefilling the rest of the address. Its flaw? They hitched their wagon to another company. If that company has flaws, then they have flaws.

In this case, Google Maps works great when it knows the address. It's a great thing to use because you're more likely to get a correct address that the customer can select rather than a customer typing something from scratch and maybe not entering it correctly. However, you have to understand how your vendor works and if there are any potential issues you might need to address.

What happens if the customer tries to enter an address Google Maps doesn't recognize? It could be a customer error, such as a customer trying to enter a delivery address that isn't recognized. It also could be a new development that Google Maps hasn't mapped yet, so it won't show up when the customer starts to enter it. However, that should not mean the customer is not allowed to get a product from you. You need to be able to handle this situation, such as the ability to enter an address freeform. It will need validation, but the benefit is that it allows the customer to continue doing business with you.

Remember that you can't always expect a perfect scenario. You have to be able to plan for the outliers as well. A well-thought-out test plan could have found this before it went into production.

# Remember That Hurricane in the News?

I've seen people decide to ignore what the data says. You can prove the data is correct if you have good data management practices. That means that you have to believe what it says.

Sometimes, people can't believe numbers are lower than they expect. They decide that it must be wrong and they have the right to change it. This is really bad when this is financial data, which is obviously a special type of data crime.

Putting that aside, there are times when they're choosing to ignore what the data means. They might have to get their noses out of their Excel spreadsheets and think about what the data means in real life.

I've seen people spawn agonizingly long research projects to find out what was wrong with a declining data trend, only to find that the reality is that the data was accurate and the decline was caused by a hurricane causing their customers, and even some of their retailers, to relocate. If you have good data management practices, don't assume that you have bad data. Accept what the data tells you, as much as you might not want to. A data trend may change for a reason and you need to act on those changes.

## Pay That Toll

I was working in a state that bordered another country, and they had a toll road where they decided to replace human toll takers with machines. A lot of toll roads have moved this way, where they can record your license plate number. They also use transponders.

Many visitors don't have a transponder but have an opportunity to pay online. The flaw in their application was that you had to enter your address information with a required state dropdown that only included states within the United States, meaning any visitors from another country couldn't pay. Bordering on Canada, where Canadians are known to be honest, people could not pay their tolls.

It was a great idea to have a dropdown to make it easy for people to pick, but it was really shortsighted to think that people had to live within the United States, especially for an area with lots of tourists. Many people build applications so that you first select country and then there's an additional breakdown based on that selection. However, in a tourist area, you might have to think if that's a good idea or if it's better to take your chances by allowing for freeform entry. Another option might have been a hybrid approach where they had dropdowns for the most common countries (the United States and Canada, in this scenario), but also allowed for freeform since this area regularly received visitors from all over the world. Do you really want to keep your toll application up-to-date on the geography of the entire world?

Another thing to consider in this situation is whether entering an address makes sense. If people can pay a toll online, an address may be unnecessary if nothing is mailed to the customer. If it's a general interest for statistical purposes, perhaps just the country could be collected.

I sometimes get really baffled wondering who's building these applications and testing them. They don't always seem to be based in reality.

## People Versus Addresses

I laughed at how they were learning on the news one night during a power outage. They started saying how x number of "people don't have power." Then they quickly corrected themselves and changed it to x number of "addresses don't have power."

While it might sound a little silly, it can really matter, depending on what you're doing. Most data modelers know how to clearly represent people and addresses. People can have multiple addresses at one time. Multiple people can live at the same address. People can move over time. All these things mean that a person is not equivalent to an address.

The easy thing to understand was how many addresses were impacted by the power outage. The more difficult thing to understand was how many people were impacted. You might be able to get data telling you who lived where or how many people were at each address. You still wouldn't know whether those people were present during the power outage or if they had visitors. At best, you could get an approximation. And then you have to question if that statistic matters or if it's sufficient to talk about addresses. In this scenario, addresses matter. In another scenario, you might have to work hard to identify people.

# Preventing Crimes Against Addresses

Addresses have been around for a long time. They're fairly stable. Countries might call components something slightly different, but they're generally the same. They might expand over time, such as when the United States introduced ZIP Codes, but even those have been around a long time. Yet mistakes are still getting made.

Address standardization is very common. It's so common that you can even get software from USPS, and other countries can have something similar. Some organizations might choose not to use it and write their own programs, and USPS publishes the rules, making it really easy. Yet mistakes are still being made. Use approved address standardization rules. Use standard abbreviation rules if you can't find them and need to abbreviate something. Those are around too. If you struggle to abbreviate, it probably means that your field lengths are too short and need to be modified. By standardizing your addresses, you can more easily reconcile identical addresses. If shipping products, you'll be able to develop efficient routing more easily.

Another shortcut people try to use is auto-completion when someone starts entering an address or a selection from a dropdown. This can be very helpful in getting an accurate address that doesn't have to rely on a customer mistyping something. The challenge is keeping it up-to-date. If a city changes street names or a new development is built, your programs need to reflect those changes in a timely manner or allow an alternate entry method.

Understanding the components of addresses is important. The common issue in the United States is people storing ZIP Codes as numeric values when they really aren't numeric. You don't need to do math on a ZIP Code, and you also don't want to lose any ZIP Codes with leading zeroes.

Understand the relationship between addresses and customers. You probably have a situation that a customer has at least one address, the address can change over time, and multiple people can live at the same address. You have to understand what happens when someone moves, how that impacts your business, and what changes you need to make as a result. If someone moves, you ideally want to update the address in one place. If you instead store the address in multiple places, you need to understand that so you can update the address in all appropriate places.

How you interact with your addresses comes from business rules – rules created by the business. There needs to be collaboration with the technology team to implement those rules. The business can't leave the rules up to technology and technology can't create the rules in isolation.

## CHAPTER 2

# Crimes Against Names

## My Name Isn't "None"

A company was trying to sell me a product and sent me an email addressed to "Hi None." Obviously, they didn't have my name, so they couldn't use it. Instead of just forgoing a name, they decided to just default it to "None." That doesn't happen unless someone programs it to do that, and I don't know why someone would think that was a good idea. Common sense should prevail.

Since it was a data management company, they made my list of products never to buy. If they mess up simple business rules, I can't imagine how they built their tool, so I wouldn't want to trust company data with this company.

It's not unusual for a company to think they should personally address a prospect, but they have to think about what to do if they don't have a name. Never forget that there might be exceptions to what you think will happen. One option would be to forgo the greeting completely. Another option would be to say "Hi." But "None" really shouldn't be the way to go. Using a default word for someone's name seems to bypass logic. Did the business approve that business rule?

# "Dear <<FirstName>>"

I got an email addressed as "Dear <<FirstName>>." To make it worse, it came from my doctor's office notifying patients about their policy around the coronavirus. I know they know my name. What went wrong?

This is another bizarre one. The doctors and nurses typically address me by name because it's obviously in my file. The email didn't address me as a blank, so someone had to go out of their way to use greater than and lesser than symbols, along with the word "FirstName" that they even used Pascal case on. Pascal case is a common standard when naming database fields, where there are no spaces but the first letter of a word is uppercase to make it easy to read. It's actually harder to do what they did than it is to get it right.

While I don't know what their thought process was in doing this, I do know that they also didn't test it. Or if they did test it, they didn't take the time to address what failed the tests. Although sending an email to all patients about the coronavirus was hopefully an isolated incident, they occasionally send emails to all patients. That tells me they must have a process for doing this, yet something went wrong here.

Getting something basic like someone's name right is so easy. There's no good excuse for getting it wrong. There are probably excuses, but no good ones.

## "Hello *|FNAME|*"

A company sent me an email addressed as "Hello *|FNAME|*." Someone actually coded that syntax! This is a data management company I've registered with, so they know who I am and my exact name. However, I suspect they've got multiple issues because they always send me duplicate emails. This time, I noticed they sent me another email with the same content, but it addressed me correctly.

I don't know how these organizations keep surprising me. Who thought coding that was a good idea? Was it a default and they thought that was acceptable? Couldn't they do better than that? I was never taught to treat data in that manner when I was taught programming. Since there were also duplicate emails, they might have received lists from multiple places where one source gave a correct name and another source gave no name, and then they never checked their master list. Even though these are just emails, and they're not paying for postage, it's still worth going through the emails looking for duplicates. If not, you wind up with situations where your reputation is at risk when customers see things like this. It's also more of a reputation risk for a data management company than a retailer, although the retailer should also get it right. Maybe they're playing a game of trying to send as many emails as possible. Some organizations think of that as a status symbol.

## Do You Change Customer Names?

Why would an organization change a customer's name without the customer's approval? Why would they transpose a customer's first and last names? Are they using some bizarre master data rules? Have they misconfigured some name standardization software?

I've seen organizations reverse first and last names, like mine. Why? If you have a file of names and the first name is in the first name field, it probably means that's the first name. There's no reason to decide to switch first and last names. Or maybe you have a list of names where the first name is always listed first. You don't then decide to take a random name and switch the order of the first and last names.

You can use some standardization for matching purposes only, like "John" and "Johnnie," but you do this to help determine if this is potentially the same customer. You don't decide to use one when the customer gave you the other. You can offend a customer if you choose an unapproved variation of a name.

You can use upper case only for processing, but again, you don't change how customers display their names. For instance, if you converted a name to "MCDONALD" and then wanted to change it back to mixed case to send correspondence to the customer, is it "McDonald," "Mcdonald," or something else?

I've watched consultants try to do this. They identified a rule in a meeting, and I saw a hand go up as someone explained that they just misspelled her name. So they said they would change the rule, and then I saw a hand go up on the other side of the room complaining that now they just misspelled his name. These are names and these are personal to people. It's one of the most personal things you have. There's no set English language rule to convert from upper case to mixed case with personal names.

If customers tell you their names, use them. When you have a relationship with customers and choose not to address them by the names they give you, it's a sure way to lose customers.

# Trouble at the Post Office

I was waiting in line at the post office and the customer in front of me explained to the employee that he was having difficulty getting his mail. Some mail wasn't reaching him and went missing or to a relative's address. The employee tried to help him but eventually said, "Do you know how many people have the last name Lopez?" Someone's got a master data issue!

From a post office perspective, this shouldn't be too difficult. The post office uses equipment to read envelopes for the ZIP Code and address. From there, an employee has a smaller set of envelopes to deliver to the right mailbox. While the employee can make some occasional errors, it sounded like the customer was having a lot of problems. Unless there were a lot of people with that last name on that street, the problem was more likely with the organizations sending mail to the customer.

Names are often not unique and organizations have to recognize that. Most use some sort of number to uniquely identify customers. If the organization starts engaging with a customer, they must make sure they're dealing with who they think they are. Rather than making assumptions, like taking the first Lopez in the list or a new Lopez must be the same as a prior Lopez, they need to ask. In this case, it was probably not this one customer who had a problem. There were probably mix-ups with other people this person knew or complete strangers. Do you want someone else to open one of your bills or receive personal correspondence? Unfortunately, we have to work with organizations to resolve their mistakes.

# "Old" Name

I guess a company messed up my account and felt a need to create a duplicate. To distinguish the two accounts, they appended one with "old." Plenty of people have done that in the past for Word or Excel file names as they're revising a document. They append it with "old" in case they need to access it again. They either eventually delete it or leave it out there in perpetuity. In this case, they did it to my name. They changed my last name to "Albert Old." When asked to verify my information when I called them, I pointed out that that was not my last name, which seemed to surprise the rep. I'm hoping he was more shocked that one of his coworkers changed my last name to "Albert Old," rather than being shocked my last name wasn't "Albert Old."

Why are they creating duplicates in the first place, and why are they changing people's names to fix their mistakes?

I'm rather baffled over what happened here. Usually, appending "old" to something means all hope is lost, and you have to start from scratch. Was that really the case here? And if so, why would you append "old" to someone's name and not some ID number? And why would you do that in a professional setting? "Old" is something I might add to a file name when I'm working on something, but it's not something that would make it to production and wouldn't be put in front of a customer.

## Cemetery Listings

Data duplication is everywhere. I was researching family history and updating a global website listing cemeteries along with who's buried there. I found plenty of duplicates in the data. For instance, someone appears with a first, middle, and last name and then has a second entry with just the first and last names. It required considerable time to fix the bad data.

Lots of things went wrong here. The important thing to remember is that we haven't always had computers. Not that computers don't have problems, but it meant that handwritten records had to be converted into something electronic. That conversion was as good as the person who did the conversion. Since I found multiple records, it likely meant that someone didn't like the first conversion and so added a different one, didn't recognize the first record as identical, or entered a record without looking to see if there was already one. These websites rely on crowdsourcing. No one is going out to all the cemeteries and uploading listings. They rely on individuals, whether locals or relatives of people buried there, to do the work. There's also no oversight, allowing anyone to make entries, right or wrong. It's nice to have for relatives who can't physically get to the cemetery, but it's also data that needs to be used with caution until you know it's correct.

# Data Quality Software

Data quality tip. If you're trying to sell data quality software to people who attended a webinar you sponsored, make sure you get the little things right. If I signed up for a webinar and know how to spell my name, but you spelled it wrong, you didn't even take it from the source. You've either manually retyped it, put it through some transformation, or applied some bizarre AI. Whatever happened, it doesn't give me confidence in the software.

Later, the same company sent me an email on October 31 saying they were "one day away" from a call on November 3. I'm not sure what math or calendar they're using, but any confidence remaining in the software was lost.

This was something odd that I experienced. I was registered with a company that produced webinars. Each webinar had a vendor sponsor. You might be there for the webinar content, but you had to realize that the sponsor received your contact information. I'm not exactly sure how it worked, but I suspect the company sent a spreadsheet to the vendor of everyone who accepted the invitation. Accepting was merely a click, so you didn't even have to reenter your contact information. Over the years, this data quality software vendor was the only one who made a mistake with my name.

What made this situation even sadder is that the vendor always talks about how they're better than other data quality software vendors because they use AI. AI can be powerful, but it's as good as the rules that someone programmed. If the rules are bad, you might as well just be guessing, which is potentially what they did with my name. Every time I've heard them talk, they gave no clarity as to what they did other than reinforcing my idea that they guessed wrong.

# Johnny Depp

Master data management came into the Johnny Depp/Amber Heard trial. There was a claim of jury fraud thinking a summons went to a man, but his son showed up instead. Both have the same name and live at the same address. The summons did not distinguish the two with an additional qualifier, such as a birthdate. Did the right person show up? The judge thought so.

Although I shouldn't be surprised by this, I am. There's no central database of names in the world that you must check before naming your child. We expect duplicate names. This was a Senior/Junior issue, although neither probably used the suffix all the time. The court has probably run into this before, recognized that it could be a problem from time to time, and had a way of distinguishing people from each other. A birthdate might have been good. I would also suspect they had access to Social Security Numbers. They didn't use a qualifier other than name.

This could simply have been a straw a lawyer was grasping at. It's also possible that the judge didn't care. Even if the wrong person showed up, there was still a jury selection process and the lawyers on both sides selected this individual. It wasn't a case of jury selection followed by a switch.

## Don't Guess at my Salutation

Another data crime is when organizations decide to ignore the data they have or guess at data they don't have. I have an ongoing issue with a global airline. Since I've flown them frequently and had issues, such as them getting my address wrong, I've had plenty of conversations with them. I found that they sometimes choose to make up a salutation for me and they sometimes use "Mr." In my profile, there's no place for me even to enter a salutation. The only option I do have is to enter my gender, and surprise, surprise, I entered it correctly.

So, if they don't ask for a salutation, why do they then need to use a salutation? Addressing a customer by the name they have, whether just the first name or a combination of first name and last name, should be sufficient. If they do decide they need a salutation and don't have one, why don't they use the data they do have? If they have gender, they could at least use "Ms" or "Mr," which will work for most cases, although there are people who prefer other salutations, such as "Dr." Again, it comes back to why they've decided to guess at the data. Overall, it feels like either a Customer Care training issue or perhaps a larger business issue where the company hasn't decided whether to use a salutation.

I assume the company thinks using a salutation is a respectful way to communicate with someone, but when they guess wrong, all they've accomplished is insult a customer or even lose a customer. With people becoming more vocal on their gender identity, this will only continue to become a larger issue. Ask for the salutation if you want the salutation.

## Incorrect Signatures

A U.S. state sent tax refunds to over 100 individuals and businesses signed by "Mickey Mouse" and "Walt Disney." These were not the names of the Treasurer and State Controller. They initially blamed it on a "technical glitch." This isn't a technical issue and is more significant than a glitch. A person caused this. They later claimed that they "incorrectly sourced" the signatures.

When people who badly need this money can't cash a check and must wait weeks for it to be reprocessed, you have seriously impacted people.

What probably happened here is they wanted to test the printing of the checks and decided to use bogus names in case the checks fell into the wrong hands. There are alternatives. They could have tested the check run on blank paper. They could have used check paper with "void" on all the checks. They could have used test names that weren't real people. At the very least, they should have had a task on their project plan to switch the bogus signature file used in the test environment with the real signature file for production. Perhaps they didn't have a test environment. Perhaps they didn't have a project plan. So many things go wrong for no good reason at all. The industry developed good organization and project management skills that need to be followed.

## Preventing Crimes Against Names

Names are personal to people and addressing someone is often your first introduction to that person. Make it a good one. Make a business decision on how to address people. That might be the full name, just the first name, using the salutation, or just saying, "Hello." Just don't guess. Don't decide to reverse someone's first and last names. Don't decide to use a nonsensical default word. I've had some organizations claim that they didn't guess, but even if it's a somewhat informed decision, it's not based on fact. If you get it wrong, you've ruined your reputation. It's better not to use a name than use the wrong name.

Some organizations use a mail merge process when they're sending mail to combine correspondence with names and addresses. This is certainly efficient, but make sure you test it first. This could be one of the reasons why mail's getting out there with default names or random programming terms. I can give some organizations a pass from time-to-time, but when they claim to be a data management company who should know better, that definitely has a reputation impact.

If you have someone's name, that's the name you should use. It's not your right to change the name. The change could be reversing first and last names. The change could be using different capitalization. If you think there might be a problem with the name, you can ask, but you shouldn't just assume it's wrong and assume your fix will be right.

Customer names are not unique. It could be common names, Jr/Sr, II/III, etc. You need another way to identify a customer. Without having that identification, you risk interacting with the wrong customer. It could be harmless or it could be personal information that gets shared. It could mean a shipment goes to the wrong person and you must replace the product. At the same time, you also have to recognize unique customers who might appear to look different because of something like a middle initial only in one record. You might have to temporarily keep them separate until you investigate and merge them.

## CHAPTER 3

# Crimes Against Phone Numbers

## Robert Frost

Apologies to Robert Frost...

Two rideshare apps diverged in a data design, and I –

I took the one that could handle a phone number change,

And that has made all the difference.

This is a cute way of comparing two rideshare apps. The issue is that when the customer's phone number changed, one rideshare app could easily accommodate the change and the other had extreme difficulties with the change. The fact is that many organizations design apps thinking that the phone number identifies a unique customer. That's not true. People can change phone numbers. New people can take over someone else's old phone number. They're not unique and they're not static.

Who is your customer? Your customer is a human being, not a phone number. If you make it too difficult for customers to change their phone numbers, they won't stick around as customers, especially when there are options, such as a competitor making it much easier.

# Retailers Identifying Customers by Phone Number

A retailer identifies customers by phone number, which we know isn't unique. If someone gives up their phone number, it can get assigned to someone new, and the new person can get an account with the retailer. The retailer considers these two accounts assigned to one phone number. The online profile does not indicate that there are other accounts connected to this phone number. It's only revealed as an issue if a cashier asks which account should benefit from the purchase. The customer is then engaged in Customer Care hell to fix the problem.

In this case, someone was a customer. When she made a purchase and gave her phone number, points were applied to her account. Then she stopped using that phone number. Either she didn't update her account with the new phone number or stopped frequenting this retailer. Perhaps she used her new phone and the retailer recognized it under someone else's name. Perhaps she opened a new account under the new phone number, meaning one person had two accounts. It's hard to know what this person did.

The other person got assigned this phone number. She set up an account with the retailer. There was no visibility that there was already an account under this phone number. The retailer found this acceptable and didn't try to resolve it. She would give her phone number when she made a purchase, yet never got rewarded with any benefits from having an account. Presumably, the other person benefited from the new person's purchases. Then one day, a conscientious cashier chose to ask her name to apply the purchase to the right account.

The customer could have left it at that, but it would have meant remembering to check which account was getting points at each purchase because the cashiers typically chose not to ask this question.

People changing phone numbers is a pretty common scenario. The retailer really needs to come up with a plan to resolve this. Even if they don't want to resolve it at the point of sale, they could at least do regular data quality checks to identify issues and resolve them.

# Bank Account Phone Number

The insurance company was supposed to give me a pandemic shelter-in-place refund deposited in my bank account or to my credit card, but they messed up and sent a check. I tried to deposit it, but mobile banking wanted to verify me through my phone number, which they had wrong.

I definitely remember putting the correct number in my account. I checked my account via my laptop and saw the same error. I fixed it there, then went back to my phone, but mobile banking still had the wrong number. I waited a day in case it needed to sync, but the problem persisted.

I checked via my laptop and it was wrong there again. I then had to spend some quality time on hold waiting for a human.

It turns out that while the website gives you the illusion that you can change your phone number, you can't and they don't give you a message telling you that's the case. You have to physically go to the branch to show ID, which wasn't great since this was during a pandemic.

It's not unusual that a bank wants to keep customer data secure. Did they accomplish that here, or did they just create unnecessary processes for the customer? I have to use my password to get into my account. Isn't it my responsibility to keep the password safe? Maybe they think someone might get my password, change the phone number, and take the money.

If they decide customers aren't allowed to change a phone number, they shouldn't allow customers to go online and change a phone number. By allowing it, customers think everything's ok until discovering that the task was not performed. That sounds like basic functionality they forgot to implement.

In the end, I went into the branch to show my ID to change my phone number in my account. And no one bothered to check my ID.

## Preventing Crimes Against Phone Numbers

The first thing to remember about phone numbers is that they're just phone numbers. They're not your customer. They're not a unique identifier of a customer. Your customer is a person who may have one or more phone numbers that can change over time. If your application doesn't recognize that a customer can change a phone number, then you've designed your data model and your application wrong.

You must have an approach for handling those phone number changes. Things aren't always going to be neat. You might be able to rely on customers to update their accounts with their new phone numbers. That's great, but you must consider what happens if you already have that phone number attached to another customer. You won't get a quick cheat sheet telling you Customer A has this new number and Customer B, who previously had that number, now has a new number as well. Multiple customers can have the same phone number, so it's not always a mistake that needs fixing. You could be proactive and search the database regularly for potential issues you might have to resolve. You could have a prompt on the account to verify with the customer whenever the next personal interaction happens. Waiting until the customer tells you there's a problem, such as missing points in the customer's account, should not be the approach.

Many organizations now use two-factor authentication, where a customer may attempt to do something online and the organization texts a message to a phone to verify the customer. While this can be a great security measure, you must remember that a customer can change a phone number. If you implement special rules to update a phone number, you have to make your customer aware of the rules. If not, the customer may be making updates online thinking everything is fine, yet finding out later that an in-person visit is required to change a phone number.

## CHAPTER 4

# Crimes Against Accounts

## Somewhat Auto-Generation

I got a letter from a bank after they linked my accounts in two countries. They had misspelled part of my address and had chosen not to use any capital letters in my name or address. When I checked online, my information was correct. When I called Customer Care, they claimed that linking accounts auto-generates this letter, but requires the agent to manually type in the name and address. So, the "auto-generation" doesn't pull from the accurate name and address in the accounts. It creates extra work, plus it creates inaccuracies. And they seem ok with it. What sort of business process is this?

When the two accounts are linked, they should contain the same address. If they don't, that should be questioned. Assuming they're the same, that would be something that could be pulled into the auto-generated letter. Asking someone to manually enter the name and address is just asking for errors. If something else was needed, they could have presented the name and address from the account and then asked the agent to click that it is appropriate to use.

Given that they decided an agent had to manually enter the information, they could have introduced a check that the manual entry matched what was on file. Since it didn't match in this case, it just makes the customer question if the data in the account is accurate and take the extra validation step.

The agent also got sloppy and entered the name and address all in lower case. Maybe pressing the shift key was too much effort. This is not professional or expected from a global bank managing someone's financial assets. Employees need to think beyond the texting they do in their personal lives and act professionally.

# I Don't Need a New Account Number

A large global hotel chain I've done business with for years decided to create a new account number for me. They transferred all my points to the new account, but none of the activity. They initially told me the activity would show within a few days, but it didn't. They kept making up different stories. One was that IT was working on it and they didn't know when it would be done. Eventually, they just ran out the clock. They only display a year of activity, so once the year had passed, it would never show up anyway.

From a data perspective, I understand what should be happening behind the scenes, so it was frustrating to find that they couldn't complete a simple task within a year. I'm not even convinced they intended to ever fix it. I think they just wanted to get rid of me and move on to the next customer. That is actually a common problem when Customer Care is rated on how quickly they address a customer call. They had the data. They proved that to me by presenting me with a very rudimentary data dump from somewhere. I don't know if it was the main database or an archive. They were unwilling to display it on the website for some reason. As I had additional stays at the hotel chain, they showed up on the website until they dropped off after a year, so the website was working as designed, except for this outlier.

## I Don't Need Another ID

I transferred cable and Internet service when I moved. The company created a new account number. They then told me I needed to create a new ID too. I suggested they could point the existing ID to the new account. They eventually agreed after a lengthy discussion over weeks.

This is a very common situation. People move. People want uninterrupted cable and Internet service. The fact that this was even a problem is surprising. As far as I could tell, the old account was associated with a special promotion and they weren't sure they could break the account from the special promotion. Their solution seemed to be for me to create a new ID, although I was reluctant to do that. I was worried it would mean they wouldn't completely close the old account and leave me paying for two overlapping accounts.

This comes down to how they designed their data model and their application. It seemed that the employees were unsure if they could do this. The data model seemed to allow it, but they weren't sure if they had the capability through the application provided to them. It eventually worked out, but it was a lengthy process. Validating data models – one organization at a time.

## Unexpected Bank Card

I was a customer of a bank for years and then closed the account. Much later, I opened an account at that same bank but at a different branch. Within a year, I received a new bank card in the mail without an explanation for why. The number was completely different, so I called the bank to make sure this wasn't because of fraud.

After some investigation, the rep determined that my previous account from years ago was due for renewal, so they discovered I was a customer again and sent me a new card. She said the card wasn't even linked to an account, so there really wasn't even anything I could do with it. Was this a bad data merge? She canceled it properly this time, or I guess we'll see in five years or so.

This seems like a situation where there were lots of opportunities to catch the problem, yet they didn't implement any of them. A customer can have multiple accounts. When the customer closed her only account, that should mean that a new card should never be issued for that account, so it shouldn't be part of the renewal process. If a customer comes back years later, a new account is opened. Even if the old data exists, perhaps in an archive, it is old and does not connect to the new account. Does it make sense to issue a card on a closed account that's been closed for years? Does issuing a card on an account with a zero balance make sense? This feels like a situation where the bank wasn't clearly thinking through all their scenarios.

# Preventing Crimes Against Accounts

Organizations often create accounts for customers. That's fine, but they need to understand the relationship between an account, a customer, and potentially other things such as an address. Whatever "account" means to the organization, there must be business rules to go along with it to identify the relationship with the organization. If you maintain a long-term relationship with a customer, you want to understand the whole history of that relationship. Creating a new account number is a sure-fire way to lose track of your customer history. If there is a reason to create a new account number, at least attach history to the new account.

Depending on your business, a customer may have multiple accounts. In that case, you need to understand what each represents and how they relate. Changing one account may or may not impact the other accounts. You have to clearly think through your business scenarios.

An account can have a wealth of information. You need to use it. It can be appropriate to validate with the customer that the information is accurate, but if you ignore the information you have and ask the customer to continually provide it, the customer might start to wonder what other questionable business practices you have.

## CHAPTER 5

# Crimes Against Products

## Embedded Logic

For people who come from a logical modeling background like I do, you know that you don't embed logic into your data. Anytime someone decides this is a good idea, it might work for some time and then fail miserably.

Every data element has a single meaning and purpose. You don't create something like an account number containing three different things that are also their own data elements. If one of those data elements changes, you must also change your account number. And that account number is probably what uniquely identifies the customer.

I worked with a company that decided to embed logic into product names. A product name was unique and may contain multiple words. Someone came up with the idea that if you used a hyphen in the product name, it was actually a different product. Otherwise, you used spaces. However, they never documented this rule, no one completely understood the rule, and the data was always wrong. It was too easy to make a mistake and put a hyphen where there should be a space. Don't do this!

# Inventory

"I'm getting two. Does it matter that they're different colors?" That's what I heard a customer ask an employee in the self-checkout line when she was getting a package of white hangers and a package of blue hangers. The employee said it didn't matter.

Yes, it matters! The product type, size, and price may be the same, but the color is different. It has a different SKU. You just messed up your inventory! And this is also probably one of the reasons why we shop at this retailer and have to keep walking around employees climbing on shelves and sitting on floors doing a physical inventory.

It would have been easier to scan both rather than wait for an employee to answer the question and then enter a quantity of two on the screen. Frankly, I don't even know how to enter a quantity unless the screen prompts that question. I would have just scanned both and moved on.

In reality, mistakes can happen and theft can happen, so it's always possible that physical inventory does not exactly match what the data says. However, you can minimize the errors by not contributing to them. By knowingly making mistakes such as ignoring the color, you're just making an existing problem worse.

## Categorizing Pizza

Some organizations find it useful to categorize data. For instance, in designing a pizza for Pi Day, you might have a dropdown for "toppings," or you might see what I saw.

They had dropdowns for size, cheese, dressing, kitchen (still not really sure what that was), meats, sauces, and "veggies." "Pineapple" was under veggies. Did they throw it in the vegetable category because they thought pineapple is a vegetable or because they just wanted a catch-all at that point?

For the record, while pineapple is not a vegetable, it is very tasty on pizza.

Categories can be helpful, especially when there are a lot of selections. However, you have to carefully define your categories so that people can find what they need. In the case of the pizza, there weren't many options, so it was not a problem to locate what I wanted. However, I have encountered some applications where I've had to go through all categories looking for something, only to find it in the least likely group.

# Data Breach Dropdown

It can be helpful to use dropdowns to control your incoming data. However, when the website has a data breach dropdown with "Equifax," "Marriott," and "other," I wonder why there's no "all of the above."

I give them credit for at least having "other." But what does "other" even mean? When you've been specific enough that you need to name the Equifax and Marriott data breaches, it seems that you really care which data breach someone was a victim of.

When you have "other," that doesn't tell you anything other than it wasn't Equifax or Marriott. It could be one of the other countless data breaches. It also might mean someone chose "other" when it truly was "all of the above." There were no rules around when you could choose "other," and there was no freeform field if you did choose it. For Equifax, it impacted almost everyone in the United States, so that doesn't qualify your data much.

## Preventing Crimes Against Products

Understanding your products is important. If you're interacting with your products and don't understand what goes into them, such as the differences between product features, you risk treating them incorrectly. Those features, such as size or color, are there for a reason and are not interchangeable.

Data crimes come from not clearly defining products. If the product seems to overlap with another product or is confusing to the customer, then the customer could have problems finding or purchasing the product. Confusion can come from embedding logic in product names or IDs, but then the logic no longer makes sense if the product changes. If the customer likes a product and then can no longer find it if the name or ID changes, you run the risk of lost sales.

In defining products, it's not unusual to categorize features. If you do, make sure that the categories are distinct and make sense. If customers struggle to find what they're looking for, they could get frustrated and move on. If you define categories with "other" or "none of the above," make sure you understand what that means. It might mean that you need to add a freeform field to collect information, or it could mean you want to ignore the other values because you want to focus solely on the values you did define.

## CHAPTER 6

# Crimes Against Defaults

## Prescription Refills

After refilling a prescription, the label said that it allows for 998 more monthly refills. Something tells me someone is using a default number in the number of refills field. Either that or they recognize my great genes.

For some reason, programmers years ago decided that using all 9s was a great idea when a value was needed and they didn't know what it was. First, you should decide if a default value is a good idea. Second, you should decide if the default value makes sense, especially if it could be real. And then think about it again if you've come up with all 9s.

There are prescriptions people need to take long term, but is it an appropriate medical practice to allow for an indefinite number of refills? In most cases, while allowing a certain number of refills is not unexpected, a doctor typically wants to see how patients progress rather than leaving them alone forever.

The patient needed regular monitoring in this situation, so getting 999 refills didn't make sense. But why did it happen? Was the doctor supposed to enter the number of refills and forgot? In that case, should the pharmacist be checking when filling the prescription? Or did it really not matter because the doctor trusted that the patient would return and the dosage would be adjusted as needed?

# Default Age

I was researching a doctor and the website said she was accepting patients from age 0 to 150 years. Darn. I guess she won't be my doctor for the rest of my life.

This was another odd default to use. Some doctors have an age specialty, such as pediatricians and geriatricians. I guess this one was trying to make the point that she could see anyone regardless of age. In that case, did an age range make sense? If so, why choose 150? Why not 200? Or the dreaded 999? Another possibility is that it wasn't her choice at all. She might have been willing to see patients regardless of age and hadn't filled out a box they needed for the website, so the website developer had chosen this age of 150.

This is a good case of knowing your business rules. The business needs to come up with the rule, such as 150 years. Then the technology team can develop it. Then the business can test it and approve it before it goes into production. Maybe this happened. Maybe they saw it and said they were good with 150 years. I still think it's peculiar.

## Preventing Crimes Against Defaults

Defaults should be used with care. If you don't know a value and decide to use a default in its place, the default should make sense. It could throw off your operations or any statistics you do if it doesn't make sense. In the case of prescription refills, I would hope this would only be a high number if it is known the patient can't get into trouble taking too much of the medication.

Identifying a default is a business decision. The business has to agree that this is a good thing to do and the chosen value is appropriate. As the world evolves, such as people's longevity, values that make sense today might not make sense tomorrow. Values that are often chosen are in the extreme and throw off averages. Values can also be chosen that fit within the designated range, thus skewing a value that isn't represented as much as it should be.

## CHAPTER 7

# Crimes Against Identifying Data

## Flight Numbers

Changing keys has always been a bad idea. You can easily lose track of your data unless you've developed a workaround solution to connect the data. Think about flight numbers. That number allows you to easily look up the history of that flight and check for things like its on-time record. It might still be the flight you must take, but at least the history tells you the likelihood of getting to your destination on time.

Sometimes though, I think the airlines want to lose history. I once worked on a project where I took the same flight every week – same airline, origin, destination, time, plane type, everything. The flight had a 100% late record. Yes – late 100% of the time! I wouldn't have thought it was possible unless I experienced it myself.

The airline changed the flight number every few months, which masked the late record and reset the statistics. Those of us sitting in the airport every week knew the truth. When you spend hours in the airport every week with the same people, you start talking.

Some people think you can always trust data. They think it must be right as long as you have data. Absolutely not. You have to manage the data properly. Trust good data, but don't automatically trust random data. Someone researching this flight probably wouldn't delve deep enough to realize how bad the on-time record was. Unless they could go further back in history, they wouldn't know the truth. The average person might research by flight number, but that would be it and they would miss the reality. Unless they knew changing flight numbers was a reality, they wouldn't check any further to see the game the airline played with the on-time/late record.

# Bad Pilots

The FAA approved the development of a database to track "bad pilots." This was discussed for 12 years, after a 2009 crash outside Buffalo. It took 12 years just to get the approval to develop a database. It meant the database still needed to be developed, which they said could take "a few more years." This should not be a difficult task. It shouldn't take 12 years to decide to make a database and it shouldn't take still more years to create one. Meanwhile, we still have bad pilots.

How did this get out of control? It's important to be able to identify the bad pilots. It's important to be able to identify how "bad" is defined. You need to make sure bad pilots don't get confused with good. But isn't there already a centralized tracking of pilots? I hope we know that the people flying the planes we're in were hired by airlines that checked their backgrounds. At the very least, someone could have kept an Excel spreadsheet, and that's saying a lot coming from a data management person.

This timeline shouldn't be acceptable. In a non-government environment, if a consulting company told the organization it would take years just to develop this database, the organization would hire another consulting company. We've all experienced bureaucracy in government, which is likely what this is, but we're dealing with people's lives.

## Credit Card Benefits

A credit card company unexpectedly sent me a new credit card with a new number. I hadn't been expecting one, so I was immediately concerned if this was fraudulent. When I questioned the company, they said they updated cardholder benefits, which required them to change the numbers for all their customers.

In reality, benefits should exist regardless of the credit card numbers. Benefits will probably change over time and you need an easy way to make the changes without impacting the customer. They likely had a poor data design that forced them into something that they shouldn't have had to do.

New benefits should have meant updates could happen behind the scenes in the database. It shouldn't have meant that they had to go through the expense of issuing new plastic cards to every customer and every customer had to update their credit card number in all the places it was stored. It was a needless disruption to customers that displayed the company's poor business rules.

# We Won't Give You an Alternate Way to Locate Your Package

A large package delivery company I worked with used tracking numbers to track packages. That's critical so people know where the package is, when it gets delivered, and if it gets stuck somewhere. They also gave customers an online application to enter the tracking number to check on the status of the package. That's critical as well. Customers can look up the package status online instead of bothering Customer Care.

They have a lot of data in their databases, but that single number was the most important thing to them. If a customer lost the tracking number, there was no way for the customer to track the package. The website only allowed lookup by that tracking number. As data people, we know there are alternate keys and ways to search for the data, but they only provided that single option both to their customers and Customer Care. IT would be able to search the database, but Customer Care wouldn't or couldn't contact them.

This lack of enhanced search capability feels like a poor business move because they must constantly encounter customers who can't find the tracking number. The customer always knows the tracking number in a perfect world, but this isn't a perfect world. Having alternate search options would have been a better design.

## Know Your Driver's License Formats

I needed to do a background check for a company that hired me. As I entered my information into the system, it rejected my driver's license. I kept getting a message that what I was entering didn't match the format for that state. The first thought was that I made a mistake, but no matter how many times I looked at it, I knew I hadn't made a mistake. I tried the obvious of substituting ohs for zeroes, but that didn't work either.

I did a quick online search and discovered that the state had changed its driver's license formats a couple of years previously. That means that the background check company had built data rules into their application so that people would enter correctly formatted driver's license numbers. That's a great idea, but they failed to stay current on their data rules. For a period of time, both formats are valid for the state, but the old format is being phased out as the licenses expire. I debugged their problem, but that still didn't help me since my information couldn't be entered. The solution was that there was a manual review to get the background check approved, but I don't know if anyone ever bothered to fix the application. This can't possibly be an isolated incident.

As I mentioned, having rules at the point of data entry is a great idea. It helps prevent bad data from getting any further into the systems and causing problems further down the line. But you have to make sure that your rules are good. If you don't control your rules, and in this case, they didn't because the rules belonged to the state governments, then you have to stay on top of any rule changes that come out so you can update the programming accordingly.

Even with monitoring rules, I still typically like to have a yearly process where I review rules. It's too easy to think that you'll update rules when something changes, get caught up in other things, and forget. In this case, I uncovered the problem in a simple Google search.

## The Car License Plate is not Unique

Don't make assumptions about data. Most people probably assume that car license plates are unique by state. Not so! It might be true in the state you live in, but not necessarily all states. Some states use plate type to make it unique (e.g., passenger, commercial, trailer, and antique). That means that someone's passenger vehicle might have the same plate number as a commercial vehicle in the same state.

For some people, this is something they strive for. They might have a number they like and get it on all their vehicles.

For some people, it's a surprise. People have been known to incorrectly get tolls or get stopped by the police because the plate type wasn't checked. There are even a handful of situations where people have been stopped and the police draw guns.

One state moved from human toll takers to machines reading the license plates, but the application they built didn't bother checking for the plate type. It meant that people all across the state were getting invoices in the mail for their little cars that had never gone over the bridge. Then they had to defend themselves to the state by showing that their little car doesn't match the invoice photo of a big rig.

Possibly, the state used an application built for other states. If the other states didn't need plate type to make the license plate unique, then it likely wasn't built into the application. It's a great example of having to know your business rules and perform effective testing.

## College Admissions

I heard a story that some colleges had accidentally sent acceptance letters to the wrong candidates. When I searched online for more information, I didn't immediately find the story because it appears this has happened for years.

One year, letters were accidentally sent to people applying for a master's program in computer science. (Is that a warning?) Some blamed it on a "computer glitch." Some blamed it on a "mail merge" or "switching software systems." And then there was one blaming it on "relatively young professionals" put into roles without much experience.

This can have a huge impact. People wait for these letters. Families gather for the opening of these letters. Videos are all over YouTube. They need to be right. How do they then tell someone an acceptance letter was sent in error? How quickly do they catch the error? The more time that goes by, the more time the student has to plan for school, which could include relocation and rejecting other schools.

This is an easy problem to solve. It's not about young hires. It's not about a machine magically doing things. It's about having the right data and the right people to treat it well. If data sets are being merged, properly test before going into production. Good data management should be a part of every organization's culture, including colleges.

# In the Navy

Where do people get their data? No – I'm not a high school senior. No – I'm not looking to be recruited into the United States Navy.

It was a text message from a Navy recruiter. He called me by a different name, seemed to think I was in high school and considering the Navy, and wanted to discuss the Navy further with me. I did some research on this one. I looked him up online and found someone by that name who was a Navy recruiter. He referred to a local high school. I decided to write back and let him know he had not reached the right person. If he had really had prior contact with her and felt she would be a good addition to the Navy, I felt it was the right thing to do.

It might have been a complete mistake by typing in the wrong number. It might have been a case of me being assigned a phone number this high school girl previously had. Either way, I let him know he had the wrong information and got a polite response back from him.

That wasn't the end. I have since gotten multiple texts from him. I haven't paid enough attention to track if it happens towards the end of the school year or if there's perhaps a recruiting period the Navy uses. However, it has been multiple years. At this point, she has surely graduated. She's either in the Navy or chose another direction in life.

He needs to consider where his information comes from because he's wasting time trying to recruit me. I'm sure I'm not the only one either.

## Search Criteria

The importance of accurate metadata. Anyone familiar with Toronto's fall/winter One of a Kind craft show knows how huge it is. During the pandemic, they went online. I quickly determined how unmanageable the online marketplace was when I tried to filter on something and got thousands of results, many of which did not match my search criteria in any way.

Any search was giving thousands of results, and there was tremendous overlap. Going by exhibitor was tricky as well with 661 of them. I decided I needed a better way.

I could download the directory into an Excel spreadsheet to filter by name and craft category, then go to the individual maker pages I was interested in where I could see things once. I could track where I had been and what I still needed to go through. It was still a lot, but 661 exhibitors was easier than the usual 1,000+, and the volume is why we love this show.

I was able to develop a workaround, but there should have been a better way. One thing I was experiencing was seeing the same thing multiple times. To some extent, that makes sense, because if they have categories like "clay" and "glass," an item made of clay with glass inserts will be in both categories. However, there was so much overlap that I think something must have been wrong with how they set up their categories. It also didn't help that the volume of people accessing the website made it extremely slow.

# Hashtags

Any other data people out there disturbed by hashtags? The idea behind a hashtag isn't bad. It can be useful to tag things and pull together that commonality. The problem is that when you have everyone in the world using hashtags, there's no way to have any control over them.

People can be careless and don't always use them uniquely. There's lots of redundancy. You make a spelling mistake and it can reference something else completely.

If you're going to use a hashtag, it doesn't hurt to check to see how other people are using that hashtag so you don't accidentally tag something completely irrelevant. I'm not advocating a "hashtag database," but just putting that warning out there. When I started #CrimesAgainstData, I checked first that no one else was using it.

## Aspirational Master Data

Mastering data can be powerful. You can do so much with your data once you've implemented all those rules and don't have to worry about which version of the data is correct. Unfortunately, many organizations only use a subset of data to feed into their master data solution. When you leave data behind like that, you haven't truly mastered the data. At best, you have aspirational master data. You hope it will be fully mastered in the future, but it isn't now, so you still have to deal with the discrepancies.

This problem often happens when an organization has been operating for years, has problems, and decides to buy a master data tool. If they don't recognize the full benefit of the business rules and tool, they might scale back on the project for time or money and only put a subset of the data through the rules. It might be the most critical data that goes into the tool, but it's not all the data. Then, if a department has been comfortably using an application for years and they erroneously think they can trust it, they will continue trusting it even if it isn't benefiting from the master data. Or if they get told their application is fine for the customer name but they have to go somewhere else for the customer phone number, they'll quickly forget if their application already contains a phone number.

We essentially have to make these applications fool-proof for people. Most people are not going out of their way to use bad data. But if you're presenting them with bad data, they'll continue to use the bad data. It's like recycling. Most people are fine recycling when they have a box at home they can put at the curb, but if you make them drive ten miles one day a week during business hours, they're less likely to comply.

## Preventing Crimes Against Identifying Data

We need to be able to identify data. We have to confidently know what we're referring to and not confuse it with anything else. We need to know the history so we know what has happened to it in the past. When the way we identify the data is changed or lost, it becomes difficult to work with the data. Identifiers should never be changed. Sequential or random numbers can be useful.

It is important to properly define identifiers. When you try to be helpful by embedding logic into an identifier, you run the risk that part of what is embedded into that identifier will change. When that happens, you've essentially changed the identifier. Unless you have an easy way to map one identifier to another, you lose the ability to track history. Again, sequential or random numbers could have prevented this.

If you're using embedded logic to validate data, you must keep those validation rules current. That can be hard to do if someone else owns the rules. If an organization in your industry owns that data, they might not consider notifying users if they change the rules. If you make an incorrect assumption about the data, you risk making a mistake and impacting your customer.

Alternate ways to identify data are also important. While they're not always unique, it can be a way to successively narrow down the options. This would be similar to geography where we can take the United States, break it down to a specific state, then a county, and then a city.

## CHAPTER 8

# Crimes Against Storing Data

## Hoarding Data

We're supposed to use the data we collect. Are we hoarding data or are we using data? I've seen plenty of cases where companies collect data and then don't do anything with this data. That's a different type of data crime because they claim they can do things with the data and then don't bother using the data.

I worked with a company that collected data every three hours on the status of their trucks around the world. However, they gave their customers access to a website that was updated every few days or weeks, rendering the data useless to customers in determining the location of the truck. Asking Customer Care where the truck was didn't help either because they also couldn't access that data.

Assuming the company did collect the information it said it did, it was just sitting in a database somewhere taking up space. It could have been valuable data. Instead, they just have no idea where the truck is or when it will reach its destination. This doesn't give the customer a good feeling.

Unfortunately, this is not unusual. Many companies collect data because it's available. Maybe data comes from your regular operational processes. Maybe there's some industry data that you think might be useful someday. Someday doesn't always come. If you have the data and aren't really doing anything with it, you may not be maintaining it properly, don't know if it's current, don't know what it really means, and have the risk of having stored this data. Are there any privacy risks you now have by keeping this data? Is there a risk someone's going to use the data in the wrong way? Data is valuable, but you need the right data.

# Hands Off!

Another common data crime is when people think they can do whatever they want with data they can access. Sometimes, organizations get data from external vendors and those vendors place restrictions on how to use the data. Maybe they're not allowed to share the data without permission or maybe they're not allowed to combine the data with other data to reverse engineer the source. Countries also restrict some data from being allowed to leave the country. There could also be restrictions on the data going to certain countries, such as those they're at war with. That includes placing it in the cloud if the cloud server is in a country it shouldn't be. There are also restrictions around marketing, so you can't just send information to customers just because you have their contact information.

These are all complications when working with organizations, especially global ones. These complications are common enough that data people are looking out for these issues. The challenge is educating non-data people in the organization who might think they're being helpful to a coworker or customer without realizing they violated a data rule or potentially a law. Before you know it, some analysis has been done that merged data in an Excel spreadsheet or a download of data was sent to a coworker in another country. You always have to make sure you're using the data compliantly, not just using the data.

## Leading Zeroes

Leading zeroes, and whether or not they get truncated, is a problem that has existed since the beginning of computers, but it has also been solved since the beginning. Why do we still have databases and applications truncating important leading zeroes, such as on a ZIP Code? Is it a training issue or carelessness?

I sometimes wonder if the ease of developing applications these days (and perhaps the desire to make their first million) is causing people to skip over the basics and jump straight to developing something they aren't ready to develop. Or maybe they make something quickly for their own purposes that others show interest in, and then it takes off before it's ready for prime time. The fact is that when there are known problems that have been known for decades, there are ways to solve these problems.

When you have numbers, there are questions you have to ask. Is it really numeric or should it be stored as character? Are there numeric leading zeroes that you must extract in a certain way so you don't lose the leading zeroes? A ZIP Code might look numeric, but you don't want USPS to find all your correspondence to the Northeast undeliverable.

## Data Lineage

If you don't have your data lineage documented, how can you test that the data is correct and prove that any reports and analytics based on the data are accurate? How can you confidently sign off on financial statements?

Your data lineage will document how your data moves and what happens in that movement. It might simply move from one database to another. It might go through some sort of transformation or calculation in that movement. It shows up on a report or in an Excel spreadsheet. If you don't know how it got there or what it went through to get there, you can't have any confidence in the data.

You also need to understand that lineage to test your data. Testing is not just about ensuring a value shows up on a screen where it should. Testing includes ensuring the *right* value shows up on that screen. The only way to know that is to create scenarios and know what the results should be. If you start with a value of 10 that goes through calculations and should come up with 20 on a report, then you must know that. If 15 appears, you've done something wrong and must fix it. A pass isn't that a number showed up. A pass is that the *right* number showed up.

## Finding Old Data

A former coworker passed years of background checks until one day. He was allowed on site at the start of a project while they went through the initial paperwork, which included background checks. No one expected any issues because he worked for a large reputable company and had already passed their background check. And then someone showed up in his conference room one day and he was escorted off the premises.

What happened was that a teenage incident showed up on his background check. He claimed it was when he was "young and stupid," but it was an isolated incident and he was told it had been expunged from his record. Was it? We surmised that someone had gone through a database conversion and something turned up that had been archived in an obscure database.

There's no way to tell with complete confidence what happened, but a bad database conversion is possible. Sometimes, older data was archived to make room for newer data and it was fine to archive data that wasn't highly used. With newer technology and business needs, people sometimes want to put "all" the data into the shiny new database. While that can be helpful, you always need to understand the data. Make sure that you're not violating any constraints. It could be something like what might have happened here when they brought back expunged data, or at least not the indicator field that it had been expunged. It could be something like bringing in private data, such as Social Security Number, that not everyone needs to see.

## Learning Path Data

I received two identical emails from a reputable data management software company congratulating me on successfully completing a learning path. I've never taken one of their learning paths. Their data is wrong. Again – they're a data management software company.

This was especially disappointing because data management is what this company does and they should know better. If something like this is wrong, how was the software designed? If I was a customer of theirs, would I have similar problems with my customer data? Can I trust that the software was designed properly? Are they using their own software?

Although I haven't taken any of their learning paths, I have talked to them before and attended some of their seminars. Maybe that somehow messed up my data with the data of people who had completed learning paths. I don't know what they did, but they misinterpreted the data. Designed properly, they could have separated people who had completed learning paths from those who hadn't.

# Variable Speed Limits

Some major cities in the United States are converting highways to "variable" speed limits. The fixed speed limit signs were removed and replaced with solar-powered signs with changing speed limits based on the traffic pattern.

Is this a case of big data or what? Are they really collecting all the data about changing speed limits and times to prove what the speed limit actually was when someone is allegedly caught speeding? And what about when the sun goes behind the clouds and the sign doesn't display any speed limit at all? Things we think about when we're stuck in traffic!

The idea behind this was that the speed limit could be higher when traffic is light on the highway. When there's a lot of traffic, they'll slow the speed limit so people should be more cautious. There's still a speed limit that people are supposed to follow. People can also be reckless. It becomes a little more difficult for the police to monitor. If a ticket is issued, people often try to fight it. When there's a physical sign, there's proof of the speed limit at the time. Where is that proof when that sign is an electronic board that can change from one second to another? It will be interesting to see how this plays out in courts.

## Retirement Money

A large global bank is being accused of losing some of its customers' retirement plans.

The customers made deposits into their retirement plans in the 1990s without any additional deposits or monitoring. Nearing retirement, they claim the money is no longer there.

The bank has gone through a merger since the 1990s. They say the records no longer exist, but the customers withdrew the money years ago and the closed accounts no longer exist.

It will be interesting to see what the truth is in this one. Is it a data issue or customers forgetting what they did over 20 years ago? What should the data retention and destruction policy look like?

I'm not sure how it's going to be solved. The customers might have a paper receipt showing what was deposited in the 1990s. Retirement money typically sits for years before we withdraw, but that doesn't mean we should completely forget about it. When people change jobs, even though they can leave retirement money alone, they are often encouraged to consolidate it into a centralized retirement plan to ease tracking. We know not everyone does that, and they had an expectation that their money was safe at the bank.

The bank claims that the accounts were closed years ago. If that is true, how can it be proven? What is the expectation for how long records should be kept about closed accounts? I believe it is far less than decades. But without that information, the bank can't prove the account was closed. Is the burden of proof on the bank to show the account was closed or on the customer to show the account was never closed? How do you show an account was never closed?

Personally, I'm a data person, so I'm on top of changes like this in my accounts. I know where all my accounts are and how much is in them. I monitor them on a regular basis. There's nothing wrong with regular statements, even on accounts that aren't regularly used. Some of my accounts have gone through mergers, and I have closely monitored the before and after. I might try to trust that they tested, but I'll trust and verify for myself.

## Preventing Crimes Against Storing Data

We say we want data and keep it, but we need to keep it responsibly. We can't keep data just because we think it might come in handy some day and then forget what we have. Part of the issue is that data can go stale and what made sense years ago doesn't necessarily make sense today. Another issue is that some data should be purged at the request of your legal department when it is no longer legally required. Keep it for the required legal time period and then get rid of it.

Another risk people have with storing data is thinking that just because they have the data means they can do whatever they want with the data. If people have unlimited access to the data, there's a risk that they could do something inappropriate with some private data or share it with someone who is not entitled to see it. If it's not organization data but instead leased from an industry source, an associated contract should tell you what you can and can't legally do with the data.

Knowing what the data is and how to store it is important. That involves things like knowing if you have numeric or character data. It also means knowing if data could be lost if you store it in a restrictive field, such as being too short. You also have to consider not what the data usually looks like, but what exceptions could look like as well.

Understanding how the data got to where it did is key to knowing if you're using it properly. You might make assumptions based on what the field is called, but assumptions aren't necessarily right. You may think the data is one thing and don't realize that a calculation changed the data before storing it in the location you're accessing.

## CHAPTER 9

# Crimes Against Business Rules

## Keep Your Rules Current

If you define data rules, make sure you keep them current. This means keeping up with industry and business changes.

If your industry has some constraints, such as privacy rules, you need to make sure you understand them and know if they change. You can't control them, but you need to abide by them. It is unlikely someone will come to you saying that the rules have changed. You are responsible for knowing what they are and whether they change. That might involve monitoring industry events, attending webinars, reading publications, and so on.

Your business can also change over time. Maybe you develop new products or acquire other companies. That could impact your data rules, so check if you need to update them. Status quo goes out the window when there's a merger or acquisition.

Regular audits would be a good idea. You don't want to be embarrassed because you didn't keep up-to-date when something changed. For instance, a driver's license format could have changed, which requires you to update your front-end application. It's nice to think that you'll remember to revisit your rules when something changes, but the reality is that you might be busy with that change and completely forget to check the data rules. A yearly reminder on your calendar to check the data rules can be a useful idea.

# Sharing School Records

Data privacy. Think beyond security and data breaches. You might have data (e.g., Social Security Number) that not everyone in the organization needs to see. You also might have data you're not allowed to share outside your organization or country (even on a cloud server). Understand what you can and can't share.

A private school hired a teacher/coach. Despite a vetting process, they later heard things about him and investigated further. They learned that this teacher/coach had acted inappropriately with some students at his prior employer. So why did they not know before hiring? It turns out that he was previously employed through the public school system where the information was known, but the private school system does not have access to this data.

The public school system knew there had been multiple issues with this person. While no criminal charges were ever filed against him, he was fired and unemployable in the public school system. It was on his record. He managed to find a loophole and get hired within the private school system. Did the public school system have rules that prevented sharing their data outside the public school system? Was the rule that they couldn't share outside the school system, public or private? Were they scared about a lawsuit if they shared the information with the private school system? Whatever the reality was, it wasn't to protect students and the offender continued to offend.

# A $900 Million Mistake

A bank employee was performing a manual transaction to pay the monthly payment on a $900 million loan. However, the employee made a mistake and accidentally paid the entire $900 million in full. The bank then tried to get their money back.

What happened? I wasn't working there, so I can't say for sure, but the first question is why this type of transaction was manual. This is quickly followed by why a transaction this size could be made without any safeguards. Could the payments have been set up to happen automatically and systematically? Could there be restrictions on how large a manual transaction could be? Could there be a separate person who validated and approved manual transactions? Could manual transactions over a certain amount trigger an alert to go through a secondary check?

There appears to be a whole lot of wrong that happened here. Either controls were in place that weren't followed or controls weren't in place.

# Flight Upgrade

Someone tried to upgrade a Coach seat on a flight to an Economy Plus seat and the airline tried to charge $770 million for that upgrade. Someone must have entered that number into a fee table. Did they not stop to think it might be unusual?

Although I heard this reported in the news as a single event, it was likely something that happened to multiple people. It's unlikely that one person tried to upgrade and someone manually keyed in $770 million.

There likely would have been either a fee table with a standard upgrade price, or a standard calculation to determine how much each upgrade should cost. We've probably all seen what seems like random prices to change a flight, but there's some calculation that goes on behind the scenes. While it may appear random, it's probably a combination of a fee and the difference between the cost you paid and the current cost. This is something we need to test thoroughly before going into production. We sometimes think the prices are crazy, but $770 million crazy? Why did no one notice that?

# Bad Math

An energy provider is seemingly overbilling customers through bad math. They might round up one, two, or more cents in calculations. On average, it's about two cents a month, which is only 24 cents a year. However, they have 20,000,000 customers, meaning they're "earning" an extra $4,800,000 yearly. Bad math or fraud?

This seems like a classic, along the lines of early bank fraud, when rogue employees would take those fractions of a cent and divert them into their personal bank accounts. In this case, they were making rounding errors. The rounding errors were evident in each line item on the statement. Rounding rules are standard and they weren't always following them. Furthermore, they sometimes completely ignored the rounding rule and just added a couple of cents.

What happened? It's hard to know. Most people probably wouldn't have noticed, but I'm not exactly most people. Were they siphoning money into additional profits? Probably not. They claimed that the actual calculation was more complicated than they could represent on statements. They already used eight decimal places. They said the calculation they did behind the scenes was accurate, but what they showed on the statement made it appear incorrect. Really?! Can't customers handle a calculation? This just impacts trust.

## Fuzzy Match

"Fuzzy match" – the words that send shivers up the spine of any good data person. Maybe you use fuzzy match to try to determine someone's salutation or what household they belong in. We shouldn't be guessing at data. Guessing means you have a chance of getting it wrong. Rather than trying to guess at customer data, just ask the customer or use data you don't have to guess at.

I'm positive I've been the victim of fuzzy match. I've had too many wrong salutations for there not to have been at least some fuzzy match errors. Especially when I have an account and I can view the data they have on me, I can see that they don't have the salutation and decided to make it up.

These days, people are talking more about AI. "Fuzzy match" may not be used as much, but AI has the spirit of fuzzy match with hopefully some logic applied to it. However, you're still not basing it on fact, so it's probably best not to do it and risk losing a customer.

## Olympics Countries

You think you know the definition of "country" until you watch the Olympics Opening Ceremonies and see some unexpected countries. Most organizations have some situations like this with the same term meaning different things to different departments.

In the case of the Olympics, they have specific rules around defining what a country is. However, we usually have our own presumptions about what a country is, which might not match their definition. Unless we recognize there can be differences, we're making incorrect assumptions.

I usually say that an adjective can be your best friend. In this case, we have to think not of countries, but "Olympics countries." With that qualifier, we realize we must look at the Olympics' rules to define countries.

Many organizations have similar issues that could be as serious as the definition of "customer." When different people or departments use different definitions for the same term, you will have problems communicating between people and problems consolidating data organization-wide. If you have to use the same term, which is often the case, don't forget the qualifying adjective.

## Olympics Medal Counts

As the Olympics came to an end, some people were trying to track medals won over time. This can be challenging when countries change over time in name or boundaries. Take care in tracking data over time because today's data doesn't always match historical data. Make sure you're comparing apples to apples.

It's not unusual for people to monitor trends over time, but those trends are based on data. You have to make sure that you have the data for that trend. If you don't, you have to make some concessions.

If you need ten data elements, but only seven of them existed 15 years ago, what will you do for the other three in your 15-year trend? It's never a good idea to guess at data because you sometimes get it wrong. Maybe the 15-year trend was a nice idea, but you have to use a shorter timeframe because of when the data exists. Maybe you need the 15-year trend, but change the analytic to only use the seven data elements you have consistently.

## Not a PCP

After getting a flu shot, where no one checked my ID, I was happy to get an email confirming it. It said a record had been sent to my PCP (Primary Care Physician), but it was not my PCP. It was my dermatologist, so at least a name I recognized. Of course, I called to question this data issue. It seems that the PCP, who they never verify, defaults to the last doctor who prescribed you something.

To start with, I know it was just a flu shot, but rules are rules. I had insurance that allowed me to get a free yearly flu shot. By not checking ID, I could have given any name and then the person with that name could have gone in and found they were not entitled to a flu shot because the records erroneously showed they had already had one.

But back to the data issue. Some insurance companies require you to identify your PCP and some don't. Mine doesn't, so they didn't have her name. Rather than asking me if I wanted a record sent to my PCP, where they could have asked for her information, they instead decided to just send it. That might be ok because it saves them time, but what do they do when they find no PCP? One option would be to just not send it to anyone. That's not the option they chose. They decided to send it to the last doctor who had prescribed me something at that location. In this particular case, it was my dermatologist. There was no harm, other than this message that comes through from the pharmacy that the doctor's office can ignore. It's just noise to them.

This is a good example of business rules. Did the business decide that it should be done this way? Did IT decide to code it this way because the business hadn't given them specific instructions and they didn't want to ask? What if the PCP had retired? Where would that electronic record have gone next? When you create your business rules, you need to think not just about the ideal situation, but also about all those exceptions that could and will occur.

## Gas Costs How Much?

A gas station showed a price of $.699 per gallon, last seen in 1978. It was supposed to be $6.99. It wasn't a glitch, as the company initially claimed. Someone programmed it that way. It was probably an honest mistake, but clearly no one checked it before it went into production.

We've all driven past gas stations with a displayed price and then driven past it a few hours later with a different price. Gas stations need a way to easily change the prices with confidence that there's no mistake. Those mistakes can be very costly.

Does the head office set the price? Does each station set the price? Who enters the price? Who validates the price? How does the price get from someone's head to the pumps and the large message board above the gas station or the one you drive by along the highway? With a price of $.699, the company lost a lot of money, especially because there wasn't an easy way for them to fix it quickly. You need to make sure your rules are accurate and you need a way to maintain them.

## Utility Usage Starts at 0

A utility company sent me a bill with an outrageous amount. Upon investigating, I saw they started the reading at 0, instead of the actual reading based on the prior owner's usage. Did they think I wouldn't notice? And then they tried to say it was an estimated amount. Did they think I wanted to pay for at least a year in advance?

This should never have been a problem. We all know that properties can change hands. No one knows that better than utility companies. Setting up utilities is one of the first things that happens. I'm unsure why they ignored the prior owner's usage.

Some people choose to pay the exact amount. Other people choose to try to evenly distribute their utility charges throughout the year, which means there are estimated amounts until the company can do a reconciliation once or twice a year. I assume that's the reason they tried the story that I was paying an estimated amount. The problem with that theory was that the amount was so outrageous that it was comparable to paying more than a year all at once. It also missed that they started the usage at 0 rather than the usage at the time of the home's sale. They just didn't look until I questioned their theory.

Once I pointed out their error, they noted it and said they would resolve it. It still took them months to resolve, but it was eventually fixed. It also shouldn't have been the customer who found the problem. I wonder how many other customers have had a similar problem without noticing.

## Election Ballots

Someone discovered an error when voting. When I looked online for more information, I saw that this wasn't the first time something similar happened, so it was difficult to find the actual story I was looking for.

Someone was voting in a 2022 election and saw 2018 candidates on the ballot. The error was confined to a subset of cities in the state and Spanish-language ballots on touchscreen machines. Paper ballots were unaffected, as were English-language ballots.

The error was blamed on a third-party elections software vendor. Their only job is elections. What did they do wrong? It feels like one of those errors where it takes more effort to get the data wrong than right.

I suspect they were probably keeping multiple files – one English and one Spanish. When the 2022 election came along, they might have decided to start with the 2018 file and update it for 2022. That might have worked, but they only did it on the English file and forgot the Spanish file. Hopefully, it's something they learned from and won't do again. More likely, since elections don't happen every week, they will forget and make the same mistake again in four years. Then again, it's an elections software vendor, so they should have this perfected by now.

# Preventing Crimes Against Business Rules

Businesses aren't static, meaning their business rules aren't static. Major business events, such as launching a new product or participating in a merger, can impact the rules. Those rules should be evaluated and potentially updated during the event. They should also be evaluated and potentially updated on a regular basis, like an audit. Even a yearly review is preferable to ignoring them. If you're trying to produce trends on data, you have to ensure that your trend time period uses identical business rules.

You have business rules for a reason, so you need to understand those rules. You must understand what you can and can't do with the data. Making incorrect assumptions can mean that you handle the data improperly.

Understanding business rules means that you can often program them and make them automatic. That can be efficient, but also risky if they're not accurate. You also need to account for data other than the norm. Suppose you think abnormal data will never show up. In that case, you've probably guaranteed it's coming tomorrow. Never ignore the importance of testing that your business rules are functioning correctly on your data.

If your business rules involve guessing at data, even if it's an educated guess or you call it AI, you run the risk of getting the data wrong. If that wrong data impacts the customer, you can risk the customer relationship. If you're not certain about the data, it might be best to wait until you have more information for accurate data.

Departments within a single organization can use the same term to mean different things. Communication can be fine within each department, but it becomes problematic when data needs to be consolidated enterprise-wide and you don't understand all the different meanings. What can be helpful is to use a qualifying word and clear documentation.

## CHAPTER 10

# Crimes Against
# the English Language

## Words Matter

Configuration matters. Words matter. A company sent me a coupon for a free item "up to $6.99." Nice! I went to the store. There were multiple brands, sizes, and flavors that complied with the coupon. I chose an item that was only $5.99, so they were getting a deal from me. I went to pay. The cashier said the coupon wasn't accepted because it wasn't $6.99. I reminded her it was less than the value of the coupon, so the coupon should work. She tried to comprehend "up to." Then she eventually overrode the system. She was likely just trying to get rid of me at that point.

Offering free items to your customers is great, but make sure you properly configure the system and make sure your employees understand the terms.

As written, the coupon was valid. Is this what the business intended or did they program the application incorrectly? "Up to" is common English language, so there should have been no confusion, although the cashier was even confused. Listing SKUs was likely impossible because of the product variety. Configuration and lack of testing were likely what went wrong.

## Consuming Data

At some point, tech people started talking about "consuming" data or having a "consumption layer" in their architecture. That's a bit of a pet peeve of mine. We might be using data, but are we really consuming it?

Merriam-Webster tells us that means "to do away with completely – destroy" or "to spend wastefully – squander." I like to make use of my data, but I don't squander it. I want the data to be available so I can use it repeatedly.

I don't know how this terminology started, but I've seen this sort of thing before where someone takes a real English word and starts using it for something else. We see it all the time in the data world, and that's why we have to make sure that everything has a clear definition. In this case, there was no good reason to start misusing this word.

## Master Data Versus Mastered Data

If you're not mastering the data and don't have any plans to do so, do you bother calling it master data or is it just data? I'm concerned that calling it master data gives people confidence in it that it doesn't deserve. Just because it's master data doesn't mean it's mastered, and I don't think everyone understands or hears the difference between an adjective and a verb.

Everyone has master data. That's not a surprise. Your customer data is master data. Did you bother to master it? Can you tell that one Bob Smith is the same or different from another Bob Smith? If you can't, then you haven't mastered it. But it's still called master data.

It almost feels dishonest to talk about master data when people might not understand you or think you said mastered data. It's completely different. Saying you have master data is like saying the database contains data. It's a fact. The act of mastering the data is not always a fact. That takes effort.

For the non-data person reading this who doesn't understand it, that's the point. We shouldn't be using words that make it harder for people to understand.

# Election Day

Take care in the words you use and inform people of the correct definition. Take "Election Day." It's not just a single day and it's not the same as having a decision that day.

Although a little funny, and a bit sad, it's true in the United States. People hear the term and think they're going to a polling station that day to elect someone that day, but the way elections have evolved means that the election process is different than it used to be. There's advanced polling for people who will be out of town on Election Day. Some states might allow elections through the mail or online. It can also take time to count votes and respond to challenges, which also extends that single day.

It's a great example of metadata. We want to have terms we understand that have a single meaning. We want to reduce ambiguity. We don't want people to be interpreting the data wrong. The easier we can make this for people to understand, the easier it will be for everyone. At best, it's "Last Day of Voting."

## "Past Due"

If you sell your car and buy a new one, an insurance company won't charge you any extra during that policy period, but will tack on a "past due" amount to your new policy. When pressed for details, because the customer knew she had paid in full, they explained that "past due" is just the wording they use when a policy increases and they decide not to charge the customer extra at that time. Terms and definitions are important!

If the amount isn't considerably different, and the policy ends soon, it's probably not worth the insurance company's time to bill for and collect an extra amount. Adding it on to the next scheduled policy renewal seems a completely acceptable business decision.

What seems odd is to call it a "past due" amount. "Past due" is kind of a loaded term. People see that term and think it means they've done something wrong and missed a payment. They're worried they're being charged interest for missing a payment. They worry about their credit rating. There doesn't seem to be a good reason to upset your customer. In this case, no harm was done. However, using less awkward wording might have been more customer-friendly. It seems like it would have been simple to address and prevent calls from worried customers.

# A Cat is Not a Dog

A woman flew with her cat from the United States to an international country. Partway through the trip, she was told the CDC rules had changed and she couldn't bring her cat back. After reading that the CDC policy was actually about dogs, she contacted the airline to remind them that she had a cat. After several discussions, it was determined that the airline's "computer system cannot distinguish between a cat and a dog." They had chosen to ban all animals.

Wow. Is this the ultimate battle of cat people versus dog people? Was a dog person offended and programmed the airline's application to ban all animals? There are lots of animals that fly, so perhaps they don't want to list them all, but cats and dogs are pretty common. There are lots of controversies about animals on planes, "emotional support" animals, safety of animals, etc., but this was a clearly written CDC policy. They did not ban all animals. There was a specific illness that dogs might bring back from that country that they were trying to prevent getting into the United States.

Regardless of whether or not you agree that flying internationally with her cat was a good idea, she obeyed the rules. She then found herself stranded because the airline was erroneously denying her cat entry and she wasn't leaving her cat behind. Once she discovered the truth, she then had to find an airline employee willing to read the policy and work with her to solve the problem.

## "Holiday Grapes"

The grocery store had three sections of grapes labeled red, black, and green. The prices were different. I chose the red grapes. Attempting to pay, the red grapes rang up at a significantly higher price than advertised. When I questioned it, the cashier said I didn't have red grapes, despite the color – I had "holiday" grapes. Also, she had been saying the same thing all day to other customers. You need to categorize your data correctly, like your grapes.

When I looked at the package, I could see she was right that they said "holiday grapes" on them. The unfortunate thing is that the section of grapes did not have a section for holiday grapes and did not have a price label for holiday grapes. I can only assume they felt there was something special about holiday grapes that made them more expensive than the matching red grapes. It was an issue because the employee said she had been saying the same thing all day. Was the price difference between holiday grapes and red grapes worth it to the grocery store with the time they spent having employees explain the issue to upset customers? Was there something so special about holiday grapes that they could have placed them somewhere away from the red grapes? When the holiday grapes looked just like the red grapes, there was bound to be a problem. They also never identified which holiday.

# Preventing Crimes Against the English Language

Words are important when we're working with data. Proper use of the English language identifies how to use the data properly. When the words aren't clear or are misleading, it can lead to unexpected results working with the data. The issue could be with how we name, describe, or interpret something.

Too often, people don't take the time to write definitions or create documentation because they think, "It's obvious." It might be obvious to the person who created it, but that doesn't mean it's obvious to everyone. It also might be obvious until the person forgets or leaves the organization.

Sometimes, the business has an intent of what they want to do. If the business does not clearly communicate that intent to the technology team, it might be implemented incorrectly. By explaining the intent and testing before implementation, the business can have confidence that the customer will get what's needed.

Often, real English words get used to mean something completely different, whether in the data or technology world. This can also be something that misleads people. If you're using a word differently than the way it's used in the dictionary, choose another word. When real words are used in unusual or ambiguous ways, it confuses the customer and causes conflict. We don't want to give people an excuse to avoid data due to a mental block on a word.

## CHAPTER 11

# Crimes Against Pandemic Data

## Counting Tests in a Pandemic

For people unfamiliar with data, they heard the term a lot once the pandemic started. Hopefully, it was something they understood enough to take into their daily lives. For me, with my background, I knew from the beginning we would have data issues.

In the beginning, the nightly news was reporting on the number of coronavirus tests the states reported. At one point, numbers started changing. When Friday numbers were less than Monday numbers, people started questioning what was happening. There was suspicion in the beginning that the state was trying to manipulate numbers to make things appear not as bad as they were. But, I expected this. It seemed inevitable that this would happen based on my understanding of data.

What happened is that some states uncovered an inconsistency in reporting. The states were conducting tests in multiple locations. Some were tracking the number of tests conducted. Other locations were tracking the number of unique individuals tested where some got tested multiple times. They got different numbers without a consistent definition of what they were counting.

In this scenario, some locations seemed focused on the number of tests, so they counted whoever came in to get tested. Other locations recognized that someone was getting retested after a positive test and decided not to count a retest. Was that the expectation or were they just going rogue and making their own decisions?

If your metric is the number of tests, you must understand what that means and what you can do with that information. The number of tests is helpful to the manufacturer in knowing how many tests have been conducted and if they need to start making more. But what if you're not the manufacturer? If someone has a positive test and has to be tested repeatedly until there's a negative test, has that skewed the results? As things progressed, people without symptoms had to get tested to lead their normal lives – before going into the office, before traveling, before visiting an immune-compromised senior, etc. With all of that, is *number of tests* a relevant metric? It seems that it wasn't because they eventually stopped tracking it.

Another thing wrong in this scenario is that they restated numbers without communicating what was happening. States should have told people upfront. Instead, people noticed a discrepancy, repeatedly asked for an explanation, came up with their own conspiracy theory, and the state eventually came clean a week later. It was a great opportunity for data education.

## Counting Infections

Twenty people rented a house in another state for a party. All got infected. Which state counts them? Where they live? Where they got infected (and caused community spread)? Where they got tested? Where they (hopefully) quarantined?

To have useful analytics, you need to understand your data before proceeding. Depending on the question you're trying to answer, you may have to use one data set over another, or you might have to use multiple data sets. You might also recognize inconsistencies in your data that you need to resolve before the data is usable. You might also find that you can do nothing to resolve the issues with the data you have access to. If that's the case, you need to make the hard decisions about whether or not you can proceed. Maybe you can use the data to answer different questions. Or maybe you do your best and write caveats of the reality, hoping people will read them.

In this scenario, I'm not sure who counted them. I'm assuming they got into multiple metrics. And that's ok, depending on how it was defined. If you counted the number of people in quarantine around the country, you could only count each person once.

# Consistent Definitions

When things started reopening after the initial pandemic shutdown, someone in another location (and another country) was trying to compare and asked me what phase of reopening I lived in. I told her it didn't matter much. Although the titles "phase 1," "phase 2, and "phase 3" were the same, the meaning varied by location. You couldn't get a haircut in some places, but you could drive two miles to cross a border to a state in the same phase number and get a haircut there. This is a good example when we talk about metadata and the importance of consistent definitions organization-wide.

Every organization has these problems, but not everyone recognizes them. If you stay within your department, you might all be using the same language and everything's fine. Then you talk to people in another department and accidentally find that a term you're familiar with means something different to them. Think about the poor person who has to produce a report for the whole organization and then encounters this problem. It is not the job of the report writer to figure out these issues. It's a different skill set. People have to properly reconcile the data first so the report writer can just write a report and never realize this was a problem in the first place.

It seems that anything can be a problem. I've seen lots of organizations struggle to define customer. Some of the issues there involve how far back you have to look to see when a customer last purchased from you. I've also seen organizations struggle to define employee. The issues there often happen in large organizations with multiple divisions and maybe across multiple countries. It usually involves defining people like seasonal workers, people on extended leave, and contractors.

## Age Data

With so many people wanting a vaccine once it became available, we saw people trying to jump the line when their age group hadn't been called yet. Many apps were set up to trust that people accurately reported their age, but age was not validated. Age data is available, but apparently wasn't being used.

It's a nice idea to think that people will wait their turn. Most were concerned about caring for the elderly and immune-compromised, but not everyone. Validating age could have been done at the point of entry using age data when the appointment was scheduled. Worst case, those administering the vaccine could check ID at appointment time.

We don't have to be constrained by the data we create. We can purchase data, or we can make use of publicly available data. These are options open to everyone. Maybe this was not a widespread problem, so they chose not to do anything about it, but it seemed to be dramatic and always make the nightly news.

## Differing Business Rules

Once some vaccine registration systems figured out how to check age, their next challenge was that they sometimes chose to do it after someone had a confirmed appointment. To make it worse, rules could sometimes vary within the same state. For instance, someone 65 or older might get a confirmed appointment that was canceled later that day because they made the appointment through the city site set up for 75 or older. What made this so sad was that it seemed that these web designers were making our seniors debug these systems, and the seniors were the ones typically least comfortable with this technology.

This shouldn't have been difficult. There were only a small number of business rules. You couldn't even use the argument that the applications needed to be established quickly. Vaccine development took about a year, so it was eventually going to happen that these applications were going to be needed. The specific business rules, such as age ranges, weren't known until towards the end, but the application could have been designed to be ready for them once finalized. I've always believed in data-driven applications, not programming-driven applications. If you're data-driven, you don't need to keep changing program code when business rules change. You can just change the data, such as we have a 75+ age group and then later change it to 65+.

# The Importance of Defining Terms

An important part of data management is defining terms. The same holds in vaccine distribution. As people got over their distrust of vaccines and wanted one, they were trying to figure out how to get one. Could they trick the system to jump the line?

One region was ready to vaccinate "people with chronic conditions" and "other at-risk populations," but didn't define those terms.

When you don't define your terms, people will use their own definition, or what they want your definition to be. This increased calls from people trying to see if they qualify. It also resulted in people showing up for appointments and being turned away because they did not qualify. It would have saved everyone some time if it had been clearly defined.

## Addresses at Doctors' Offices

With the chaos of different vaccine distribution rules per state, many doctors' offices were sending patients emails with scheduling information. Some of them were sending messages to all patients, regardless of where the patients lived. This just contributed to the confusion when patients in another state saw an email telling them to schedule, but all the communication they heard from the state they lived in said that they didn't qualify yet.

This had an easy resolution. The doctors' offices keep records of patient addresses. Use them! The data is available for use.

I always wonder why some of these things happen. Is the program written by someone who lives in the state and can't conceive that patients don't live there as well? Did a business person share this business rule with the programmer? Did they decide that it was just easier to program it this way because the patients in other states were anomalies? It would be interesting to know what goes on in the mind of someone who does this.

## Centralized State Database

After getting vaccinated, the state kept sending me postcards about the importance of vaccination. Did I just identify that they don't maintain a centralized database? Or are they just trying to keep the post office in business?

Over time, I think we've all seen things like this. We think of the "government" as if it's a unified organization with different departments that talk to each other. The reality is that there are lots of instances of these siloed databases that don't connect to other silos.

In its most basic form, they needed to connect the list of all residents in the state with the list of all vaccinated residents. At the time, vaccinations were being done at state-run sites, or at locations that were submitting data to the state. The connection was possible, but not done.

## State Vaccination Registry

As the pandemic progressed, some people were walking into vaccination clinics, claiming they hadn't had a shot, and getting a third dose, which hadn't been approved at that time. Is there no registry to check or is no one bothering to check? Are we collecting unwanted data?

As I pondered that, a story hit the news that some vaccination clinics weren't uploading their records, so people going to the state website for proof of vaccination weren't finding their records.

After hearing that, I decided to go to the state website to see if it had my information. I had to enter my name, birth date, and ZIP Code. It then wanted to verify me by texting a phone number that wasn't mine. I had not changed my phone number since starting the vaccination series. I have no idea where they got this number. The doctor's office confirmed the correct number and the state didn't give them the option to update the phone number, so I was forced to deal directly with the Department of Health. I was left with fixing the department's data before they would tell me what was on my vaccination record.

The idea of a state registry was a good one. They seemed to think they had one because they directed people to check vaccine registration there, but they seemed not to be too careful in using it. Did they not communicate to vaccination clinics that data needed to be uploaded? Did the vaccination clinics decide they didn't need to upload the data? Whatever the cause, the data was not current. They also seemed to put security measures around accessing vaccination records, which is good, but if the data is bad, people can't access their own vaccination records. It's definitely a process that needs some work all around.

## Changing Definitions

When you define your business terms, remember that you're not done and still need to monitor them. Definitions can change over time as the business evolves. Like "fully vaccinated." That definition changed whenever a new dose was recommended.

To any data person, this one was pretty obvious that it would be a problem. We could see maps on the news showing how many people in each country were fully vaccinated, but as more doses came out and the maps never reset, it was obvious that they had become useless.

When a business defines terms, it's important to revisit them whenever there's a significant business change to see if anything needs updating. The reality is that if there's a significant business change, people are probably engaged with that and don't think about making time to look at definitions. In that case, put a yearly task on your calendar to review definitions. The review should be a much easier task than when you wrote the definitions in the first place.

## Dating Metadata

I've always advocated maintaining effective and expiration dates with metadata because things can change over time. You may have to go back in history to look at how you defined something or find what code values were valid in the past. You may need to future-date some changes to prepare your applications, like the definition of "fully vaccinated," which changed over time.

When the vaccine was developed, we saw people tracking vaccinated versus non-vaccinated. At that time, "fully vaccinated" meant that single dose. When the second dose was developed, some people still hadn't had the first dose, so what they were tracking became more complicated. Then a third dose came out. At that point, it was believed that there would be an annual shot in the future, like an annual flu shot.

As the number of fully vaccinated individuals increased, but the number of people with three shots remained low, it was hard to tell what they were recording. The only thing I was confident about at that point was that the definition of "fully vaccinated" didn't exist anymore and they should just stop reporting on it.

# Future-Dated Vaccination

Always validate your data! Someone went to get a booster and was denied because her vaccine card said she wasn't due yet. It said her second dose had been given in 2031, when it should have been 2021, so it was accidentally dated ten years in the future. She was then denied until her card could be corrected, which was a better option than waiting ten years.

On one hand, this was simple because someone actually wrote 2031 instead of 2021. On the other hand, it wasn't that simple because there was no way of knowing if that was the only error. If there were supposed to be a certain number of months between doses, how do they know that the month and day were right? They might have been wrong as well.

This type of situation then puts the individual in paperwork hell. She has a paper card containing the wrong date. The information does get uploaded to a computer application, so she then gets to spend some quality time with the government obtaining that information. Assuming that was manual entry, even if the person manually entered it with 2031, it could probably be validated through the entry date. The only challenge would be that government applications aren't always the most sophisticated.

## Your Dinner Needs Good Data Too

A state's Department of Health sent texts to 3,300 people just before Thanksgiving saying they had been in close contact with someone who was COVID-positive. They later realized they made a mistake and blamed it on a "technical issue." How many Thanksgiving dinners did they send into a spin?

At one time during the pandemic, a positive test meant that you couldn't fly and you shouldn't be around other people you could spread it to, especially elderly and immune-compromised people who you would see at Thanksgiving. People who took it seriously and got tested before Thanksgiving would have to change plans with a positive test result.

This type of thing is serious enough that extreme care needs to be taken. There shouldn't be a risk of there being a "technical issue." They also never explained what the technical issue was. Without knowing what happened, they gave people no assurances that it wouldn't happen again at Christmas or any random day.

## Insurance Refund

Since people stopped driving at the start of the pandemic, my insurance company was giving money back as a "shelter-in-place payback." Yes! They said they would reimburse you through the credit card or bank account they had on file, regardless of how you paid for the insurance. So, if what they had on file was incorrect, the money goes where? For people who have closed credit cards or bank accounts, were they monitoring for error messages? No, they were not.

They tried to tell me they put my money in my closed bank account. The bank confirmed that is not even technically possible and the insurance company has my money. After I brought it up, the insurance company sent an email saying they reprocessed the credit. One line in the email said they issued a check and one line said they deposited it in my bank account. When I checked my bank account, it showed a deposit of $0. I'm not sure that's technically possible either.

The money eventually showed up via check, but not without effort on my part.

The main thing to remember here is that data isn't static. It was great that the insurance company was offering money back, but they can't assume that the financial information they have on file is accurate unless they check it. As time passes, data can change. It probably needs to be verified. Maybe they took the approach that they were willing to assume the risk that some money went to the wrong place. Was the time it took to log the customer calls and investigate the cases worth it?

# Bankruptcy Emails

As organizations started "repositioning" themselves after declaring bankruptcy during the pandemic, they emailed their customers to announce what they were doing. When it's a big organization with multiple brands, you would think they would figure out that the same email address doesn't need an email for every single brand. I think one organization sent me six emails within one hour, all with the same wording.

On the one hand, it's just an email. They're not paying postage for six letters instead of one. But it does clutter an email box. It makes for more things I have to pick through to get to the real messages.

On the other hand, it tells me something about the organization. By declaring bankruptcy, they often plan to continue operations in some capacity. If they can't figure out that six people are actually one, what else can't they figure out? Do they have private information on me, especially financial information, that I now need to be concerned about because they don't have good data management practices? Maybe how they're treating customer data is telling me how they treated finances and this contributed to the bankruptcy.

## Defining a Customer

How do you define a customer? I watched my email volume go up at the start of the pandemic as organizations sent messages saying they were having reduced hours and then sent messages hours later saying they were closing temporarily. Then the messages came from organizations that could continue in a reduced capacity.

A clothing chain emailed me about still being able to mail orders, but the email came from a specific store over 1,000 miles from me. I also got messages from the store less than ten miles from me. When I contacted the store far from me to find out why I was suddenly getting messages from them and if my account was messed up, they said they were sending messages to everyone who had ever shopped there. I've traveled a lot. I've shopped in a lot of places. I'm sure I've shopped there, but that was years ago.

Organizations need to do a better job identifying their market. How long after a purchase do you still consider someone a customer?

Many organizations recognize the value of storing people as people. If you do that, you can associate as many relationships to them as you need to. Someone might be an employee and a customer, so there's no need to store identical names and addresses in multiple places.

If you need to contact your customers, how do you pick them? Do you look for people who have made a purchase in the past year? Two years? People who have a membership with you? People who gave you an email address? What if there are multiple stores? Does it make sense to send communications based on which stores the customer shopped at or the store closest to where the customer lives? Customers who shop at multiple locations don't need identical communications from multiple locations. The business rules must be carefully thought through before jumping and taking action.

# Rent Relief

A state started a "rent relief" program during the pandemic. Renters who found themselves unemployed could apply to the state for reimbursement of rent payments. However, the state later discovered that they made rent payments to people who don't live where they say they do. Owners/property managers say the state never checked with them to verify the renters live where they do. This should have been something that could easily have been achieved through data.

I like to think that this happened because the government was trying to respond quickly to help people in an emergency. It was something no one had experienced before, people lost income without warning, and everything was more expensive. I still think a little more care could have been taken. I don't think they needed to launch a multi-month investigation into each application, but they should have had access to check a minimal amount of data automatically and could zero in on the ones that needed more investigation. Plus, the rent relief lasted for months, so they had plenty of time to correct things if they made an error. I've said it before, but I think this is another example of government departments not talking to other government departments. The data is there. They just need to share. Once the money goes out, it's hard to get it back. It turns into a legal mess.

## University Program Average

Do you document your calculations and define your terms? With the 2020 chaos at universities because of the pandemic, some decided to just let students choose a credit/no grade rating in a course rather than a percentage. If they chose that, especially in a course they were struggling in, then that course wasn't part of their overall program average.

That meant that potential employers comparing two fairly equal students might not realize that one has an average consisting of all required courses in the program and one has an average consisting of only a subset of required courses. If you just look at the average, you might erroneously think they did equally well in the same program.

People are so used to thinking about what a program average means, so this is something different people have to recognize. Years after graduation, you can look back on it and realize it doesn't really matter, but for a new graduate, that number is important to people. It's the old analogy of whether you're comparing apples to apples or apples to oranges.

## Data Trend Breaks

Analysts can get stumped when their hypotheses don't match the data sets. They might complain that the data is bad. Sometimes it is, but sometimes it's not the data's fault. Analysts might expect a trend that isn't there. Maybe a major storm impacted the population and sales they were looking for shifted to another location where people took shelter. You must apply context to the data if you're looking for trends. How about 2020? Now there's a data trend break.

Whenever you have a hypothesis, you have to realize that it might not be right. The hypothesis will be proven or disproven through your analysis. Trying to predict a trend is just a prediction, although hopefully an educated prediction. It is not necessarily reality.

Most people had not predicted what started in 2020 – the shutdowns, the supply chain issues, the worker disruptions, the war, etc. These factors often impacted trends, so whatever you predicted had to be re-examined. It's not always as easy as we'd like. And it's not always a little hiccup that goes back to how it was.

What happens going forward? Will people remember what happened or return to assuming a trend will always match reality?

## Preventing Crimes Against Pandemic Data

Ok – I'll say it. I hope I never have to write a section like this again! I did because the pandemic had a lot of data crimes. While we hopefully won't go through another pandemic, I think we can learn from what we went through. I think many data crimes came from people acting quickly in a crisis and not stepping back to realize they know this. There was nothing really new that couldn't have been handled as if it was just another data project.

Communication is always important. People were scared. People didn't know who to believe. If you make a mistake, own up to it. If you have to restate numbers, tell people. Transparency is critical in establishing trust.

Communication of rules is also important. When multiple people need to follow the rules, they all need a common understanding of those rules. During the pandemic, some of the common issues we saw were how to count tests, how to count infections, and how to count customers. It's not that any one definition was wrong. Each definition could serve a certain purpose and solve a particular problem. When someone is trying to consolidate at the state or national level, they need to know the intent. They need to know they're comparing apples to apples and not apples to oranges.

Validation was another point of failure. The validation wasn't always performed as effectively as possible, especially with the vaccine roll-out based on health and age. There was data available that they didn't always use. They often relied on the honor system, which isn't always the most effective method.

Knowing your customer is always important. This could be knowing where the customer lives, or just knowing if this is someone you want to identify as a customer. The approach many organizations seemed to take was "everyone," which led to confusion. Pandemic rules differed by state, so if the customer was in a state other than the state the organization was in, the customer sometimes got misinformation.

There was a belief that data, such as vaccination records, could be consolidated at the state level. That was a good idea, but it needed the appropriate follow-through. Every facility that gave injections needed to send records, and accurate records, to the state website. It needed to be updated in a timely manner. There had to be a way to easily resolve discrepancies. There was probably some state reporting that was done pre-pandemic and they could have leveraged ideas, or even program code, from that.

Definitions can change over time. We saw that with "fully vaccinated," but that happens in normal business operations. People need to be aware that they need to monitor their definitions, and if they need to change, keep track of what definition was used when.

People often like to produce trends on data. When doing that, you have to make sure you're comparing identical things. It can be something like we collect more data now than we did in the past, so we can't do a trend on data that doesn't exist. It could also be a large disruption, like an organization going out of business or a global pandemic completely uprooting the world.

## CHAPTER 12

# Crimes Against Using Data

## Citizenship

The state sent postcards to non-citizens telling them they may be eligible to vote if their citizenship status had changed. So, we now know that they haven't mastered their data or they would have this information.

This is something that I've always found curious. We think of "the government," but it doesn't act as a single unified organization. I compare them to a national organization where we expect that the national organization has some level of data consolidation at the national level. And yet a lot of that is missing from the government. We hear plenty of times on the news about a criminal getting away because one department knew the person was a criminal but wasn't sharing that information with other departments.

Things like citizenship and visa status are important to track. You're entitled to certain things under one status and not entitled to other things. It impacts voting, crossing borders, and employment eligibility. This isn't one of those things you should mess up.

## Begin and End Dates

Begin and end dates can be helpful in a data design. For instance, if there's a status that can change over time, it's helpful to know when the status changes. Also helpful with road signs. For instance, seeing a sign saying "end blasting area" tends to imply that there was probably a "begin blasting area" sign somewhere. Hopefully.

Learning that I had been in a blasting area was a little alarming, but I made it through safely. I also assume it was probably far enough away from the road that it never would have been a problem. Just don't go off-roading.

The value that the dates provide is immeasurable. From a data perspective, this is the data that truly matters. The reality is that people often want to avoid the dates and think, "Just give me the status." It can be helpful to think you can just go to a status field to determine whether your customer is active. If you rely on an "active status" field, is it up-to-date? Is the definition of "active" that was programmed the same as your business definition of how you use "active"? Too often, status fields just aren't kept current.

Another great example of using dates is with new products. You're about to launch a new product. You don't want people ordering it before it's ready, but you also want to be ready at launch. You don't want to be ready to sell and then be waiting for someone to load the database. A better option is to load the data ahead of time with the date when it will be active. It also allows you to "expire" products you no longer sell while keeping the history that it was sold in the past.

# Flag

Any other data people out there questioning the unnormalized American flag? Whenever you add a new state, you need to add a new star.

Ok – I'm not saying a new flag needs to be designed, but it is an example of data normalization. When creating data models, we strive to break down the data into its components. We look for what makes the data unique.

For the American flag, it is a well-known flag, but it has changed over the years. The changes are close enough that we all know whose flag it is, but there's a date range for when the flag is used. That date range tells you how many stars it has.

Right now, it's a well-organized, symmetrical flag. Where would they add one more star? You know that state is going to want their star.

## Trillionaire

A $20 investment in a cryptocurrency seemingly turned a man into a trillionaire overnight when he checked his balance. The organization called it a "display error." A display error could go either way – positive or negative. And they expect people to trust them with their money?

This wasn't a widespread problem, although it might not have been isolated to a single individual. Did people only experience it if they checked their account at a certain time?

Does calling it a "display error" make sense? That would mean that the computer program would read "$20" and display "$20,000,000,000,000." Would someone have programmed that? Another possibility is that it was a data problem. The data might have been stored wrong and displayed as-stored. We'll likely never know what happened, other than the organization didn't let him withdraw a trillion dollars.

## Latest Billionaire

Someone tried to withdraw $20 from her bank account at a global bank and discovered her account had $1 billion in it. Trying to be honest, she was then faced with automated phone system hell trying to get a human so she could resolve the issue.

This is another odd one. This wasn't a "display error." The bank was seriously telling her she had $1 billion. The bank likely had a maximum amount you could withdraw per day, but how long would it have taken without her help for them to register that she didn't really have $1 billion?

The customer did the right thing. She really had to. There must have been cameras, plus audits, so it's expected that someone would eventually have found the problem. She likely would have been charged with fraud if she had kept the money for herself. Unfortunately, organizations make it so hard for us to contact them, so she wasted plenty of time trying to inform the bank of their error.

## Governing Data Sources

Have you ever built your data governance organization by data source instead of business function? I've seen organizations that focus heavily on external data sources, but there's so much overlapping data that they need input from multiple business functions. Governing by data source rarely works. Monitoring data quality as data is received should not be confused with the governance of decision making and rules identification.

When large data sets come from vendors and are used by a limited number of people, it can be easy to think you need a single person to manage each data set. However, if you think about the fundamentals of data governance where you have shared decision making across the organization, that same essence has to come to all these data sources. There's probably some common data, such as customer data, in multiple data sources, and we all know that data that's supposed to be identical isn't always identical. Different departments have different uses for the data. Different departments have different interpretations of what the data means. Different departments have different meanings for data quality.

If you're properly governing your data, your data governance organization has responsibility over your data sources. Individuals do not own them.

# Data Cleansing

I was working with an organization that had bad data and they hired a consulting company. Rather than fixing the data at the source and preventing bad data from entering the system, the consulting company came up with a "data cleansing" effort where they would run weekly programs to check the data followed by people fixing the data weekly. Without being fixed at the source, the bad data came in weekly and was manually fixed weekly. Over and over again. Did they really believe this would work or was the consulting company trying to keep the cash flowing?

They downloaded the data and spent time analyzing it. They were able to identify things like missing data and incorrectly-defaulted data. Their analysis allowed them to identify existing data problems and write reports so those problems could be displayed to be fixed.

The fixing part is where they went wrong. Typically, "cleansing" is a term we use when we're moving data from one database to another in the process of decommissioning an old database. Even in that scenario, you want to address why the data was bad in the first place so you don't repeat the problem in the new database.

From an operational perspective, you don't want cleansing data to be part of your operations. You want to address why these problems happened in the first place and fix that cause so the problem doesn't keep happening. Over time, you should see fewer and fewer problems displayed because you corrected them. New problems would be ones you hadn't dreamed of.

In this scenario, the consultants got good at recognizing they had fixed something the week before and remembering what they had done to fix it. But they had to do the same thing week after week. Nothing was satisfying about the job to want them to stay there. The client spent way too much money on this level of expertise. The consulting company had a regular flow of income.

# Buying a Customer Master

A company decided to fix its customer data issues by buying another company's customer master. What they got was another company's customer master, not their own company's customer master. They still couldn't reconcile it to other customer data they had. They made their problem worse.

I'm not sure what they were thinking, but I'm assuming someone heard the term "customer master" and didn't understand the concept. When I first talked to them, they kept talking about how proud they were of their new customer master, but nothing else they said about it made sense. Once I learned the details, I discovered that all they had done was contract with another company to get their customer master. There were regular updates, but that still didn't help them.

The company had a customer database but always had issues matching a customer to sales. IT recognized that a customer master could help, but rather than working with the business to develop a customer master, they thought buying one would work. They focused on it being a technical problem they could solve by loading a data set. The result was spending just as much time trying to reconcile data because another company's customer master still didn't match with their sales data. They spent a ton of money, signed a multi-year contract, and hadn't impacted the problem at all.

The ultimate solution wound up truly understanding what a customer master meant and investing business time in developing one. Once implemented, it fixed problems overnight. They had a consistent view of customers that exactly matched their sales.

# Preventing Crimes Against Using Data

We have lots of data. The problem is that we're not always using it or using it properly. When you interact with a customer and that interaction proves that you didn't pay attention to the data, you risk your reputation. Customers can ignore some things, but too many problems may put all business practices into question.

Consistent usage of data is also important. Customers don't want to expect one thing and get another. They should be able to expect to use the data in the same manner and get the same results. They'll start questioning what else hasn't yet been found when unexpected things happen.

Preparation of data is important. If your business is offering something new or changing something like pricing, you can be prepared for those changes and have them timed to go live at a designated time. You don't want to be live, have customers ready to go, and then delay things when your databases and applications aren't ready.

Hand-in-hand with preparation is data testing. This is not testing that clicking on a screen takes you someplace else. This means testing that the right data shows up in the right places. Without being properly tested, you can get unexpected results.

Proper governance of data doesn't mean one person dictating control. Proper governance means involving the right people, including representation throughout the organization. Different people interact differently with the data and those differences are key in determining the appropriate data usage for the organization.

Solving the root cause of data problems is critical. Addressing a problem as it comes up and typing over the data to what you think it should be is a way of guaranteeing that you'll never be done with this problem or possibly run the risk of financial crimes. Fixing the cause of the data problem will fix it in the right place once so it doesn't happen again.

## CHAPTER 13

# Preventing Data Crimes

Data runs the world. We use data all day every day. We use it for operational functions. We use it to make decisions. We need it to be right. When it isn't, it can lead us in the wrong direction. If we find out it was flawed, we may have an opportunity to redo our work. If we never learn it was flawed, we may have gone down a path we should never have taken and have difficulty getting back.

Properly managing data is essential. While this isn't a data management how-to book, I would like to summarize some common problems people make with data that lead them down the path of data crimes.

## Data Management

Just because you have data doesn't mean that you're properly managing that data. Managing data is a specific skill set that is learned. You can't just tack it on to someone's existing job. If people already have demanding jobs and then they get told they need to take on numerous tasks to manage the data, it will turn into something they do only if they have time. And they probably won't have time. Your data needs to be important to you, you have to have people managing it, and you have to have tasks as part of job descriptions. If you have data problems and can solve them at the source, you'll have fewer data problems over time, making using the data consistently easier.

## Communication

People must understand the data they use. You can't hide behind a single person understanding, or hopefully understanding, something. Knowledge needs to be shared with the people who are using the data on a regular basis. Without the knowledge of what the data means and how to use it compliantly, you're guaranteed that something will go wrong.

## Business and IT Collaboration

Business and IT both have roles to play. The business knows the rules, whether they realize it or not. IT implements those rules. They need each other and need to be guided by someone with data management knowledge. Thinking you can shortcut the process by eliminating certain people often leads to unfortunate circumstances.

## Data is Real

Data comes from some place. Keep data for a reason and don't keep any data in violation of regulations. Make sure it's understood and don't take actions that make it more confusing than it should be. Managed properly, data is accurate. There's no good reason to ignore it and decide that it must be something different. Used incorrectly, you run the risk of insulting your customer and damaging your reputation. With the power of social media, this reputation loss can be on a global scale.

## Exceptions

Data doesn't always do what we expect it to do. It's also not always the data's fault. When people interact with data, they can do unexpected things to the data. When you have applications interacting with data, you need to think through the data that should be there and the unexpected data you might get. While you might not think through every scenario, being prepared for some of those unusual cases can make you more responsive and lessen the risk of getting embarrassed in front of your customers. Over time, you'll have more scenarios covered and fewer exceptions.

## Data in Motion

Data represents things in the real world – like your customers and products. Those things can change over time, so your data can change over time. The business rules that act on the data can change over time. Data is not static and you need to be able to accommodate those changes when they happen. You could also implement regular reviews throughout the year to identify the changes you missed and address them there.

## Testing

Proper data testing is critical. Testing is not about taking a file from production, running it through your application, and making sure the results match what is currently in production. You need to think through all the data scenarios you might see. You might have data in production to support the scenarios or you might have to create the data. You have to plan what the results should be and then prove that you got those results. It's standard testing of a hypothesis. You hope your hypothesis is right, but it might not be. It's better to find out during testing than a customer finding it in production.

## Diversity

When we think about diversity, we often think about things like gender, race, etc. Those things can impact your data, as well as how you treat your data. Another thing to think about is how organizations often function globally. The data in your country is not necessarily the same as the data in another country. Even within the same country, such as the United States, data can vary by state. The data you typically interact with may not be representative of all the data you need to handle. If you don't understand the differences in that diversity, you might mishandle the data.

## Ethics

You need to be in compliance with the law, regulations, and contracts. However, just because you have the data doesn't mean you can do anything you want with the data. Just because you can do something legally with the data doesn't necessarily mean it's ethical. Like a lot of things, think before you act. Is this something you would be comfortable talking about in open court? Is this something you feel comfortable telling your mother you did?

## Think

Use common sense. Before you do something with the data, make sure it's something that makes sense to do. Would you be happy if someone did that to your data? If not, then you shouldn't be doing it to your customer's data. We often wind up with laws and regulations just to enforce common sense.

## CHAPTER 14

# Closing Remarks

Are you experiencing data crimes that can help you understand what an organization is doing and help you get it resolved?

Crimes against data are all around us. If you're a data person, you see them all the time and you're a victim of some of them. As a victim, you can help people understand what the issue is and how to fix it. Sometimes, I know exactly what is happening, but general Customer Care representatives aren't necessarily aware of data and the problems it can cause. I sometimes have to lead them down the path of what the problem is so that I can get to the right person who can fix the problem.

Seeing and understanding data problems in your personal life is important because this is where it comes alive. You're experiencing a problem and you understand how it feels. You are living the problem and seeing how it gets resolved. You can take that experience to work and extrapolate what is happening with the business data.

I'm a data person. I work with organizations to help them solve their data problems. But I'm also a customer. As a customer, I want them to improve my data so I don't have to suffer through the problems they create. It's somewhat self-serving.

Let's learn from the data mistakes of the past and prevent them from happening in the future.

# About Merrill

I call myself a data person. There was definitely education involved, but I also believe I was born this way. That is why I'm constantly seeing data problems in my daily life and understanding how an organization got itself into that mess. Convincing a random help desk representative of the problem can sometimes be difficult, but it eventually gets solved.

Education-wise, it started at the University of Waterloo. I have an Honours Bachelor of Mathematics degree, with a major in Operations Research and a minor in Computer Science. During that program, I learned about good data design. They hadn't yet identified all the disciplines we think of today, but the underlying structure was there, even if the terms weren't. This is also where I learned data modeling. It was the purist form – learning data modeling from a tool-agnostic view. We weren't constrained by how a tool vendor does something. I could take my knowledge to any vendor, and did.

After graduation, I did what we all did with a BMath degree. I became a Programmer/Analyst. Although it wasn't my ultimate dream, it does give street credibility. Although I only did it for a couple of years, it did help me experience the problems developers face when they don't have good data to work with. From there, I got a job as a Data Modeler, then Data Architect, and then the world of data management was wide open to me. For the most part, my specialty has been data governance, where I govern all the data management disciplines, so this pulls everything related to data altogether.

As new developments came along in the data field, people often turned to me to figure it out. In most cases, these concepts, while new in name, were not new to me in what I was doing. Data governance was a new concept, but at the same time, I had been doing a form of it when I was data modeling. I had to because I had to juggle people from across the organization telling me what they thought the data was for and what it meant. I had to bring people together and negotiate deals. MDM (master data management) came along and I realized I had been doing that too. While I didn't have fancy tools, I had to architecturally design it and build the data rules because those fancy tools hadn't been invented yet.

Now, I help organizations understand what data management means, what problems they have because of it, and how they can implement it. The goal is to better manage your data to drive value from the data.

# Index

www.ingramcontent.com/pod-product-compliance
Lightning Source LLC
Chambersburg PA
CBHW071245050326
40690CB00011B/2265